Creating Inclusive and Engaging Online Courses

ELGAR GUIDES TO TEACHING

The Elgar Guides to Teaching series provides a variety of resources for instructors looking for new ways to engage students. Each volume provides a unique set of materials and insights that will help both new and seasoned teachers expand their toolbox in order to teach more effectively. Titles include selections of methods, exercises, games and teaching philosophies suitable for the particular subject featured. Each volume is authored or edited by a seasoned professor. Edited volumes comprise contributions from both established instructors and newer faculty who offer fresh takes on their fields of study.
Titles in the series include:

Teaching Entrepreneurship, Volume Two
A Practice-Based Approach
Edited by Heidi M. Neck, Candida G. Brush and Patricia G. Greene

Teaching Environmental Impact Assessment
Angus Morrison-Saunders and Jenny Pope

Teaching Research Methods in Political Science
Edited by Jeffrey L. Bernstein

Teaching International Relations
Edited by James M. Scott, Ralph G. Carter, Brandy Jolliff Scott and Jeffrey S. Lantis

Teaching Marketing
Edited by Ross Brennan and Lynn Vos

Teaching Tourism
Innovative, Values-based Learning Experiences for Transformative Practices
Edited by Johan R. Edelheim, Marion Joppe and Joan Flaherty

Teaching Sports Economics and Using Sports to Teach Economics
Edited by Victor A. Matheson and Aju J. Fenn

Creating Inclusive and Engaging Online Courses
A Teaching Guide
Edited by Monica Sanders

Creating Inclusive and Engaging Online Courses

A Teaching Guide

Edited by

Monica Sanders

Faculty, Georgetown University Law Center and Senior Fellow, Tulane Disaster Resilience Leadership Academy, USA

ELGAR GUIDES TO TEACHING

 Edward Elgar
PUBLISHING

Cheltenham, UK • Northampton, MA, USA

Published by
Edward Elgar Publishing Limited
The Lypiatts
15 Lansdown Road
Cheltenham
Glos GL50 2JA
UK

Edward Elgar Publishing, Inc.
William Pratt House
9 Dewey Court
Northampton
Massachusetts 01060
USA

Paperback edition 2023

A catalogue record for this book
is available from the British Library

Library of Congress Control Number: 2022932893

This book is available electronically in the **Elgar**online
Political Science and Public Policy subject collection
http://dx.doi.org/10.4337/9781800888883

ISBN 978 1 80088 887 6 (cased)
ISBN 978 1 80088 888 3 (eBook)
ISBN 978 1 0353 1346 4 (paperback)

Printed and bound by CPI Group (UK) Ltd, Croydon, CR0 4YY

Contents

List of figures   vii
List of tables   viii
List of contributors   ix
Foreword   xiii
Preface   xvii
Acknowledgements   xxiii

1   Introduction to *Creating Inclusive and Engaging*
     Online Courses   1
     Monica Sanders

PART I   COURSE ACCESSIBILITY AND COPYRIGHT

2   Democratizing course access   11
     Eileen Young

3   Considering copyright in your courses   24
     Raven Lanier

PART II   THE TEACHING AND LEARNING EXPERIENCE

4   Inclusive course design   37
     LiAnne Brown

5   Accessibility tools   58
     Monica Sanders

6   Managing pace and workload in online courses   71
     Susannah McGowan

7   Apps, tools and assignment ideas for online engagement   88
     Monica Sanders

8   Developing and incorporating impactful library
    research guides for online and hybrid learners   103
    Ladislava Khailova

Appendix I: Notes and additional resources for inclusive,
    engaging online course design   120
Appendix II: Copyright checklist   123
Appendix III: ADAA   132
Bibliography   134
Index   141

Figures

2.1 Accessibility coding   21

3.1 Duck wearing sunglasses   28

3.2 Creative Commons licenses   30

4.1 "Diversity Wheel as used at Johns Hopkins University" is licensed under Creative Commons Attribution 4.0 International   38

4.2 Graphic representation of Maslow's Hierarchy of Needs   39

4.3 The Community of Inquiry Venn Diagram   40

5.1 Image UDOIT Accessibility Toolkit   62

6.1 Fall 2020: Visual of a Hyflex classroom   78

6.2 Spring 2021, sample semester by week to visualize pacing   80

6.3 Sample weekly schedule   81

6.4 Example of a Canvas Module   84

8.1 GU SCS Library LibGuide for the SCS Supply Chain Management MPS Program   107

Tables

2.1	Rich text vs plain text	19
2.2	HTML cheat sheet	20
4.1	Activity structures	48
6.1	Faculty participation in CNDLS programs	72
7.1	Animation and storyboard applications	98
7.2	Skills and assessment chart	101

Contributors

ABOUT THE EDITOR

Monica Sanders JD, LL.M

Monica Sanders is the Managing Director of the Georgetown Environmental Justice Program and holds a faculty appointment at the Georgetown University Law Center. She is also a Senior Fellow at the Tulane University Disaster Resilience Leadership Academy. Her experience as a practitioner includes serving as the Senior Legal Advisor for International Response and Programs at the American Red Cross, and as an attorney for the Small Business Administration during the Hurricane Maria and western wildfires responses. She was a Senior Committee Counsel for both the House of Representatives and Senate Committees on Homeland Security.

In her academic career, she has championed open educational resources, universal course design, affordable materials as well as diversity and inclusion in both traditional and online learning. Her approach to working with students is centered in their experiences, and influenced by practical experience in dealing with clients and communities.

Professor Sanders has designed equity themed courses and created a fully open access law casebook. In addition to editing and writing for this handbook, she is pursuing an electronic legal textbook project.

CONTRIBUTING AUTHORS

LiAnne Brown

LiAnne Brown is a senior instructional designer and learning architect with over 15 years of experience in curriculum development and course design. Ms. Brown earned her Master of Science in Education (focus on Instructional Design for Online Learning) from Capella University.

She has designed and taught several live, online, and blended learning courses and developed online and blended learning curricula in the allied health education space. In addition to teaching and curriculum development, she also served as a volunteer accreditation surveyor for the American Society of Health-System Pharmacists (ASHP) Pharmacy Technician Accreditation Commission (PTAC) and engaged in allied health education program evaluation across the United States. She also authored a Pharmacy Technician practice textbook for Elsevier Publishing in 2012.

Her course design and teaching background, along with the facilitation of Intercultural Competence workshops for higher education faculty and staff, have informed her perspective on the cultivation of inclusive learning environments for adult learners. Her design philosophy is based largely on social constructivism that is centered on learners engaging in collaborative events of instruction to build meaningful social learning connections. The cultivation of inclusive learning environments is vital to adult learners making learning connections that will translate into long-term behavioral growth and change.

Ladislava Khailova
Dr. Ladislava Khailova is the Director of Georgetown University's School of Continuing Studies Library. Prior to her appointment at Georgetown, she was a Professor at Founders Memorial Library, Northern Illinois University, serving as a humanities and social sciences subject specialist and the coordinator of library services for persons with disabilities. She also taught American literature and English composition at South Carolina State University and the University of South Carolina.

Her previous works in this area include the book *The Stories We Share: A Guide to PreK–12 Books on the Experience of Immigrant Children and Teens in the United States,* which was published by the American Library Association in 2018.

Raven Lanier
Raven Lanier is a Copyright Specialist at the University of Michigan Center of Academic Innovation (CAI). In her work at CAI, she has helped hundreds of faculty navigate the copyright issues that come up when creating massive open online courses, credit-bearing online degree courses, and other forms of online content. She manages a small team of students that reviews third-party content used in CAI supported online

courses and has created a variety of practical guides on how to thought-fully use the copyrighted works of others in online courses.

Part of Raven's role is based out of the U-M Library Copyright Office. Her work at the Library Copyright Office focuses on making copyright law engaging and understandable, consulting with faculty and students on copyright issues, and helping the U-M community find and leverage open and Creative Commons licensed materials.

Raven received her J.D. from the University of Michigan Law School and is a member of the Michigan State Bar.

Susannah McGowan
Susannah McGowan is the Director for Curriculum Transformation Initiatives at The Red House at Georgetown University. Previously, she served as the Associate Director for Curriculum Design at the Center for New Designs in Learning and Scholarship (CNDLS). After starting her career in educational development at the CNDLS from 2001–2007, Susannah earned a Ph.D. in Education and worked at University College London and King's College London in England. While at King's, she co-established King's Academy in 2017, a center for educational development supporting integral programs for faculty and graduate students around inclusive pedagogy, assessment, and blended learning. She has worked as an advisory fellow of the John N. Gardner Institute for Excellence in Undergraduate Education, a nonprofit organization dedicated to improving equity and student success through course design innovations. Her research interests include threshold concepts in disciplines, students as partners work, and sustainable educational development as a driver for institutional change.

Eileen Young
Eileen Young is a PhD student in the Disaster Science and Management program at the University of Delaware. She graduated in 2016 from the University of Wisconsin at Whitewater with a Bachelor of Science in Liberal Studies and in 2019 from the University of Delaware with a Master of Science in Disaster Science and Management. She is currently engaged in research using agent-based modeling of social factors in evacuation from fire. Her interests are in collective behavior, resilience in vulnerable populations, and the evolving role of computing and big data in social science. Her work has included data analysis to support

the Federal Emergency Management Agency (FEMA). She also has an ongoing interest in inclusive, accessible learning environments.

Foreword

As we wrote this foreword, our home university – Arizona State University (ASU) – re-opened the fall 2021 semester for in-person learning. Orientation events were held across campus and students and teachers returned to campus with both enthusiasm and hesitation. Students, particularly graduating seniors, were relieved and happy to be back on campus so they could have one last year or semester in-person among their peers and with a professor in the classroom. Although most instructors missed the in-person experience, too, some worried about their health, potential exposure and impact on their families and loved ones. ASU strongly recommended vaccines and required face coverings in certain indoor spaces but it was up to individuals to act responsibly. At semester start, we were in the throes of a third wave fueled by the Delta variant resulting in around 3,000 new COVID-19 cases daily, that largely infected unvaccinated and younger populations. If 2020 taught us anything, it was that we needed to be prepared to pivot back to remote learning, and to be able to do so seamlessly, effectively and expeditiously. We had to design our fall 2021 courses for in-person learning but with options for online learning modality at the ready.

At ASU, we have a substantial online infrastructure and presence. Several years ago, we shifted the way we think about teaching and learning and embraced technology. Technology-based teaching tools were not merely an add-on modality; they became, instead, the foundation for a new and truly integrative teaching and learning experience. Online learning and online degrees make higher education more accessible, inclusive, and equitable. A degree program that is completely online is an appealing option for students who cannot afford expensive out-of-state tuition, student housing and transportation. It is useful for students with families, full-time jobs or who are serving in the military, returning to school to finish a degree program or seeking a career change. It can be a godsend for someone who must stay home to care for a sick family member.

Access to and institutional resources for remote learning, however, remains uneven. Our institution had several years to bolster the digital infrastructure, train personnel, provide free software and digital storage tools, and create support services that include 24/7 counseling, and time management and success coaching. COVID-19 and the global shutdown forced faculty to move their teaching and student interaction online within a matter of weeks. Faculty had to quickly learn the basics of virtual meeting platforms, online quizzes and exams, AI-assisted reading annotations, augmented and virtual reality applications and real-time polling in class. Faculty had to learn how to create voiceover slide presentations, video recordings and to make adjustments to course assignments that worked differently in an online classroom. It was a world foreign to faculty who marginally utilized Blackboard or Canvas or never pursued training in online instruction. Some found online teaching overwhelming, time consuming, difficult to learn or confusing. Not all instructors mastered online course design or knew how to engage different learning styles among a student group in a virtual classroom.

Students were also forced to pivot quickly to a new way of learning, engaging with their teacher and classmates, and adapting to a new delivery system for information. Some students thrived and appreciated the opportunity to learn from home, while others struggled to maintain interest in the work and engage effectively with the teacher and the class. It was not uncommon for "A" students to suddenly miss class regularly, show up on Zoom unprepared or to show little interest in earning good grades.

When in-person ASU classes transitioned to fully online in March 2020, the inequity in access to basic tools to do online learning were evident, particularly among communities of color. Students who ordinarily relied on campus computers were shut out when the libraries closed and everyone was expected to work from home. Students who returned home to shelter safely with family suddenly found themselves competing for bandwidth and home computers with siblings who were also forced to homeschool and parents working from home. Many students relied on the internet available on their cellphone to engage their classes but not everyone had or could afford the appropriate data usage or service plans to adequately get classwork completed. Eventually, ASU provided laptop and hot spot loans to students through the campus library.

Native American students at ASU were hit particularly hard, as many of them returned to rural reservation communities to be safe with family. Rural reservations, more often than not, lack adequate broadband infrastructure (Running Bear et al., 2021). Before COVID, reservation residents regularly accessed the internet by using free Wi-Fi at popular retail outlets like McDonald's. Internet access via cellphone is popular although limited since strong cell signals are unreliable in remote areas. It is not uncommon to see reservation residents parked on hilltops or special spots where they know they can get a signal. Public libraries were helpful for people who lacked both computer and in-home or cell phone Internet. COVID-19 closed public libraries, limiting even further the opportunities for students and workers to stay connected. COVID-19 revealed compelling disparities in access to health care, food, safe drinking water and communication. The impact of the virus on the Navajo Nation, for instance, was felt immediately with high numbers of citizens contracting and succumbing to the illness. Many Indian nations closed their borders in an attempt to curtail the spread of the virus and everything – work, school, health care delivery – went online.

Cost is a compelling consideration for online education. Not all institutions have the resources or personnel and students to make remote or hybrid teaching successful and economically sound. Small colleges, tribal colleges and resource-poor institutions may struggle to make the necessary investments to include a digital learning platform as an integral part of their programs. Will we see a disappearance of smaller colleges, or will small schools with in-person instruction become a luxury for the 1%? Will schools with strong online degree programs use those revenues to stabilize exorbitant tuition and perhaps offer financial aid, and thus access, to first generation students or students from underserved groups?

Our ever-changing world demands universities and instructors to be creative, adaptive and resilient. The usefulness of remote learning is not limited to emergency situations; it also offers powerful ways for us to connect students with people and places all over the world, important when such opportunities are limited due to cost. Not all students have the resources to study abroad or volunteer work that shows them the world. The technology means we are not limited to the knowledge delivered in a physical classroom. It can be a valuable tool but we have a responsibility to ensure that no one is left behind.

Universities must provide technological and pedagogical support so instructors are proficient users of online teaching tools and they know how to adapt online learning to meet the needs of their students. Instructors are the key to ensuring equitable access to remote teaching for our "return to normal". Our new normal will likely blur the lines between in-person and remote learning and will change the way we think about, plan, train for and implement curriculum and the teaching and learning experience going forward. Blending the two modalities, even for courses advertised and offered in-person, is likely to become permanent. After all, there will be another pandemic, another hurricane, another economic downturn; whatever the situation we need to be prepared.

This book offers compelling examples and is an excellent resource for course designers and instructors. The authors go beyond idealizing the benefits of online learning. They are instructors and practitioners who purposefully design inclusive and engaging courses – an essential mindset for online teachers at any level of learning.

Michelle Hale Assistant Professor, American Indian Studies, Arizona State University and Melanie Gall Clinical Professor, Co-Director Center for Emergency Management and Homeland Security, Arizona State University

REFERENCE

Running Bear, C., Terrill, W. P., Frates, A., Peterson, P., & Ulrich, J. (2021). "Challenges for rural Native American students with disabilities during COVID-19". *Rural Special Education Quarterly*, 8756870520982294.

Preface

This handbook started out of necessity. The COVID-19 pandemic forced educators at every level from the familiarity of classrooms and laboratories into a fully online environment. While some had experience in online or hybrid learning, accommodating large and diverse classes of students was a new experience. Transitioning classes from a written syllabus into an online creation of similar quality was daunting. Continuing to do so for more than a year was something beyond imagination.

Drawing on my own experiences during the pandemic and from previous experience with online learning, it seemed the time was right to move forward with creating a tool to not only make delivering online courses easier, but also an engaging experience for both the student and educator. Just prior to the pandemic I had begun working on an inclusive and accessible course design project in response to what was then a global conversation about the "digital economy" and the changing nature of education and work. At that time, the issue was about thinking about access and equity. When we design spaces, particularly learning spaces, for whom are we doing the work? The answer should be "everyone".

Intersecting with conversations around the digital economy and how to prepare for it, were conversations about digital society and citizenship. In the United States and several other countries protests and calls for social justice and inclusion added additional layers to how we conceptualize learning and pedagogical approaches, particularly online. If the economy becomes digitized and the remainder of society is to follow, then how we design rules for participation in that society should be parallel with preparation. Developing hard skills in students to adapt to online learning and other online spaces is not sufficient. Developing critical thinking, adaptation and citizenship skills are part of online learning as much as it has been in the traditional classroom. A core part of that is embedding representation, equity and inclusion into the digital learning environment.

Because this handbook was devised and created during the COVID-19 pandemic, the authors frequently reference the impacts of this period in world history. While I and my colleagues are champions of inclusive, engaging and accessible learning, some of us also work in the realm of emergency and disaster management. That is the "black line" job, helping communities understand, prepare for and recover from catastrophic events. One thing a person learns working in this space is that these events do not create hardships or inequities, they simply amplify them. In this sense, the pandemic was no different.

COVID-19 challenged societies and institutions to consider how to address a variety of inequities that are barriers to student success, including: poor Internet access, sharing space with siblings also learning online, and for some, without having accessibility tools. Intersecting with these challenges were discussions about representation and inclusion. These are difficult topics in a traditional classroom, but amplified in the two-dimensional realm of online learning. Upon receiving a grant to do an inclusive online course design, I ventured to create a course that could be accessed from a phone and had materials that could be downloaded to make learning in areas of low connectivity easier. I also wanted to create spaces where a variety of students felt comfortable, included and ready to engage as digital citizens.

In creating this book, I had the pleasure of working with a diverse and extraordinary group of women. Each brought their own unique perspective about pedagogy, inclusive course design and even how to address copyright issues so that creation, innovation and imagination can continue to be a core part of online teaching and learning. Every contributor has a passion for online teaching and learning. Each has experience in discrete areas such as digital design in addition to inclusive online learning.

We set out to create a handbook for innovative online course design that can work for any hybrid course, taught partially in-person and partially online, flex classrooms with a mix of students online and in-person as well as fully online and asynchronous (self-paced) courses. This book is divided into two parts. The first part will cover how to create a course that is easy to navigate and mobile friendly, incorporates inclusive design to foster acceptance and community in diverse students, as well as accessibility features to meet accommodations. The second part will focus on the teaching and learning environment, specifically how to incorporate digital learning tools, guides, applications and other resources to make teaching and learning in an online environment pleasurable.

ABOUT THE CHAPTERS AND APPROACHES

As mentioned in the discussion about access, being accessible can mean having the ability to provide courses and adapt the learning environment to crises. But it can also present a unique chance to reach an almost unlimited number of students with an almost unlimited variety of materials. Understanding this ongoing set of opportunities is what inspired the layout of the book, but particularly the first section which includes course access and copyright as the core topics.

Chapter 1: Introduction to *Creating Inclusive and Engaging Online Courses*: Per the conversation about digital economy leading to an increasingly digital society and development of digital citizenship alongside new learning skills, I introduce this approach to the teaching and learning experience and how learning in a digital environment is appropriate for the digital age. I also discuss the benefits of "crossover" knowledge students have learned from gaming, social media and use of apps that are conducive to enhancing learning in this format. The chapter will also include an overview of equity issues in digital access, highlighting the need for a focus on equity, inclusion and access – especially in a digital learning environment. The chapter will connect the concept of the benefits of "crossover" knowledge with the pitfalls and set the stage for the conversation to be had in subsequent chapters. First, we look at course accessibility and copyright, addressing the stepping stones to building a successful class.

Chapter 2: Democratizing course access: This chapter will explore how to design courses that can be accessed and fully participated in despite different levels and modes of Internet access. Eileen Young will discuss the benefits of HTML coding versus uploaded PDFs, using online open access materials such as "remixed" textbooks rather than traditional textbooks and scanned resources and how to incorporate them in learning platforms like Canvas. She also provides easy to follow, step-by-step instructions to show faculty how to create accessible pages that work in mobile environments and adapt to accessibility tools.

Chapter 3: Considering copyright in your courses: This is a topic that we felt is under addressed in higher education and particularly in online learning. Many times professors and instructors will use a different media to add variety to their online courses. This can run the gamut from movies, videos, podcasts and visualizations to presentation tools. Often it is not clear what materials are fair use, which need permission and what kind of permission is required. In this chapter, Raven Lanier, a copyright attorney and expert, will go through different media and the legal requirements where needed and walk instructors through the process of understanding what is needed and when.

In Part II: The Teaching and Learning Experience, we wanted to make the connection between design, pedagogy and outcomes for students and instructors. In part, we ventured a deeper exploration of Universal Course Design to understand how students receive and process certain assignments and materials. This is part of our work to ensure equity and inclusion are part of the course design and development thesis we present in this handbook. There is a further parsing of the concept of "accessibility" to advance the conversation about access to include understanding different disabilities, different learning styles and incorporating a variety of tools to help accommodate them. We want the reader to understand that these accommodations do not diminish the experiences of some, but enhance the experiences of all learners.

We had more opportunities to bring in unique perspectives about online learning that we felt are not addressed enough. These are helping students conduct quality research and access research support online and understanding how to pace courses and assignments to prevent burnout and feeling overwhelmed. Not surprisingly, the pedagogical approach to this book is student-centered and inspired by Scholarship of Teaching and Learning[1] (SOTL), which views the learning environment as student-centered and focused on scholarship. This does not mean that the authors do not subscribe to other theories or believe that multiple approaches may be best. As it happens, for this handbook the process culminated in this way.

Chapter 4: Inclusive course design: LiAnne Brown takes her expertise in Universal Course Design and extends it to include representation and inclusion. Among the topics to be covered are examining ideas about racial, ethnic, cultural and religious awareness in class. That can range from ensuring representation in course materials is diverse to creating assignments that expose students to subject matter experts from a variety of backgrounds. It will also include practical tips about using discussion boards and breakout rooms for small group chats about difficult topics.

---

[1]   For notes or additional resources: https://www.researchgate.net/publication/233817081_Scholarship_of_Teaching_and_Learning_An_Overview.

Chapter 5: Accessibility tools: In this chapter, we pick up the conversation about access and accessibility. Part of the chapter will review some accessibility tools and learning management system evaluation tools. Beyond that, we will look at accessibility through a student-centered, equity lens concerning both disabilities as defined by law, but also the broader lens of neurodiversity. Here, we include tips and perspectives about how to address a variety of accessibility needs in your class. Finally, there is information about how to work with university entities like disability and student services and diversity officers. These professionals can serve as resources for issues such as customizing accessibility tools for the online environment. They can also help with understanding the universe of student needs and ways of learning.

Chapter 6: Managing pace and workload in online courses: This issue was highlighted during the pandemic as students and professors struggled to understand how to translate contact hours requirements into online and hybrid courses without exposing students or professors to burn out. Susannah McGowan, an expert from Georgetown's Center for New Designs in Learning and Scholarship, will go over how to design a course in Canvas to flow at a certain pace, how to account for adult learning principles (ex: the "50 minute" working hour) options for varying the length and format of assignments, and creative assessment options. There are charts and graphics to explain how to pace classes across different schedules and how to adapt for a variety of students.

Chapter 7: Apps, tools and assignment ideas for online engagement: In this chapter we will cover how to make online teaching pleasurable and engaging for students and the professor. The topics to be covered will include alternative presentation tools to avoid "PowerPoint" overwhelm, using Jamboard, whiteboards, Kialo and argument ranking portals to simulate the "chalkboard" experience in physical classrooms and how to create alternative assessments to gauge student progress. In this chapter we also address elements of universal design that can help with student engagement as well as enhance overall digital literacy. Similar to other chapters, scholarship of teaching and learning is referenced with respect to encouraging creative opportunities for students, but also creating community and evolving thinking about the teacher-student relationship.

Chapter 8: Developing and incorporating impactful library research guides for online and hybrid learners: Ladislava Khailova shows us how to make it easier for students to access library resources and conduct high level research in an online environment. Her expertise comes from her own work as an author and educator, but also from being the Director of the Georgetown School of Continuing Studies Library. This is a global scholarship and research environment with a large portfolio of online and hybrid courses. In this chapter, she explains the benefits of library guides and subject matter background guides as tools. You will learn how they can be incorporated into a learning portal and used as a foundation or background for a course, research or lecture starters or as review tools.

We also wanted our readers to have additional, quick access resources that can be used as quick reference tools while creating courses. There is a bibliography which breaks out all of the references in this book, a copyright checklist to keep handy, and a copy of the Americans with Disabilities Amendments Act to help with accessibility. We have a section called "Additional Resources" where you will find a detailed listing of the applications, tools and guides we discuss in the book as well as other pedagogical resources that could accompany the topics written about in this book. It is my and my creative partners' sincere hope that you find this book and the resources contained in it helpful as we navigate the evolving educational landscape.

Acknowledgements

Taking an idea from concept to reality is never easy. That was even more true going through this process during the COVID-19 pandemic. What made this necessary also made it challenging and I could not have done it without a diverse and varied support system.

To my friends and loved ones: Dakota, Kerry, Barb, Karl, Edna, Nisa, Walter, my solid congregation of cousins and neighbors, thank you for cheerleading, supplying refreshments, Zoom breaks and anxiety relieving laughs.

Many thanks to the team at the Center for Teaching and Learning at the University of Delaware. This began with their generous support of an experimental course design grant and continued with their support of their project.

Thank you to my mentors, Dr. Tim Frazier and Dr. Tammy Anderson, for helping me figure this out and for believing in my ideas about how to teach and learn.

I also offer gratitude to the Center for New Designs in Learning and Scholarship at Georgetown University for its continued support of my work and pedagogical development.

Thanks to everyone at Edward Elgar Publishing, especially Caroline Kracunas, the ever-patient acquisitions manager who guided me through this process as a first-time writer.

I would like to thank all of the contributors to this book, LiAnne Brown, Ladislava Khailova, Raven Lanier, Susannah McGowan and Eileen Young for their generous contributions of time and talent. It was a tremendous pleasure working with you and benefitting from your expertise.

Finally, but not last in my mind, to the young people in Baltimore at Sandtown and the St. Joseph's Center for your questions, determination and inspiration. It was watching your efforts to supply yourselves with the tools to learn despite numerous challenges that taught me the lesson of a lifetime.

1. Introduction to *Creating Inclusive and Engaging Online Courses*

Monica Sanders

The teaching and learning experience has evolved and continues to evolve in the wake of digital classrooms and online learning. Depending on who you ask, the concept of teaching as an art or science began with Socrates in the 5th century B.C. (Le Pôle, n.d.) or Joseph Herbart in the 17th century (Blyth, 1981). For some it is an art, reflecting the style and approach of leading one's students to education. In schools of law, Socrates' legacy is encapsulated in the Socratic method, which is about leading one's students to the truth. The two can be seen as equivalent. Those who teach need to be creative in the classroom and the process of seeking out new creative methods can be described as an art.

Others view it as a science, likening the methodical approach to teaching as a parallel to scientific methodology. The ultimate goal is not a particular view of education, but the process by which one goes about providing education. It is the science of teaching and learning how to teach, which many view as an applied science. That does not mean it is without a moral imperative. Herbart took a Platonic and scientific approach to classical pedagogy by saying the purpose of teaching is to bring about the natural talents and abilities of students. But that must be balanced against methods and the norms of "civilized society". The role of the professor is to infuse their concepts of personal maturation, which included "Inner Freedom" and "Benevolence".

This is similar to some traditional teaching pedagogies. The didactical approach is teacher-centered, with the teacher delivering and students receiving lessons and information (Tomei, 2010); an approach often found in certain areas of science teaching, but also generally predominant in some educational institutions. This is somewhat similar to what is known as the traditional method, which scholars say is teacher-centered, but more focused on memorization, recitation and retention over skills-based learning. Another approach is competency-based learning,

1

where the focus is on problem solving, critical thinking and development of different kinds of reasoning. The commonality between these is the approach: whether it views teaching as an art or a science depends on the teacher.

Alternatively, there is the scholarship of teaching and learning, which is distinctly student-centered and based on taking a systematic inquiry into the nature of student learning. It requires taking a look at the consequences of one's teaching on students. Peter Felten gives five principles of good practice in the scholarship of teaching and learning (Felten, 2013). They are: inquiry into student learning, grounded in context, methodologically sound, conducted in partnership with students and appropriately public or shared. This approach, in whole or in part, is increasingly part of modern teaching and has an influence on online learning. This is particularly true regarding the inquiry into student learning. Delivering online content without sacrificing pedagogy of any kind is a challenge; more so if you are interested in this approach. Student-focused online learning is part of an approach to help prepare students for the future digital economy. Before the COVID-19 pandemic, there was a push to re-think work and education in a world where more people were online than ever before. The World Economic Forum calls it the "Fourth Industrial Revolution", where artificial intelligence and machine learning will both disrupt and create new jobs. A McKinsey Global Institute report predicted that about 14% of the global workforce will need "upskilling" by the year 2030 (Hendricks, 2021). For those charged with preparing these new learners, online education in the economy of the future means embracing and teaching new technologies in tandem with developing online pedagogy. This means not only rethinking teaching methods and approaches, but creating a system of delivering education that accommodates the needs of a smarter, busier and more digitally savvy student body.

This need is demonstrated by the struggles online learners reported with their class experience. Etu et al. found that 75% of online learners in 2020–2021 reported dissatisfaction with their classroom experience due to the instructors' lack of preparation for teaching in that environment (Etu et al., n.d.).

For universities, this flexibility translates into more enrollment options. The National Student Clearinghouse released a report that supports the idea that COVID-19 accelerated the move to online learning. According to the report, institutions with online learning saw a 2.2% increase in enrollment during the first semester of 2021 (National Student Clearinghouse Research Center, 2021). Part-time enrollment grew by

5.1% and older or non-traditional student enrollment grew by 7.1%. Growth rates were higher in specialized and executive programs, such as online masters and business degree programs geared towards working students. This, coupled with additional research signaling an increase in higher education learners with additional work and family responsibilities, requires a new level of preparation that is student focused and works for new kinds of students. In the latter part of this book we offer concrete ways to not just address but co-create new ways of learning with this emerging student body. In the first part of the book, we deal with access and the digital divide.

When conversations about the "digital divide" arise, they are rightly focused on overall Internet access and not as much on what is *accessible* on the Internet. Of the many issues the COVID-19 pandemic exposed, the need for a variety of tools to be accessible from different devices across differing levels of connectivity was predominant. Going forward, increased online learning offerings will not diminish the necessity to think about students' need to access courses from a mobile phone using data or Wi-Fi as much as from a laptop with an HDMI connection to high-speed broadband Internet. And with this broadened access comes more opportunities for exploration.

According to the US Census Bureau, 15% of households with college and other school-aged youth do not have a high-speed internet connection at home. About a quarter of low-income families have no computer access at home. This often translates into higher use of mobile devices with limited access for live media and streaming. Roughly 17% of American teens (in both secondary and post-secondary education) are unable to do school work because of this lack of access to the Internet or a computer. As with many societal challenges, these issues are exacerbated when applied to students from marginalized groups. It is often the most documented concern in both the digital divide and accessible learning. In thinking through the design of this book, focusing on the idea that mobile access is the only form of access for many students, it made sense to encourage mobile friendly and accessible course design.

Thinking about course design requires a multi-frame thought process that questions everything from how you want your cover page to look on your learning management system (LMS) to how students will receive the material you place in that system. In this section we will explore two aspects of course design that are often thought of near the end of that process or only when there is an issue concerning one topic or the other.

Accessibility is often a reason to connect with the disability services office at one's university with the aim of serving a particular student's needs. The great shift online during 2020–2021 brought a broader definition of accessibility to light when the difficulties of accessing the Internet for purposes of online learning were revealed. Online learning can open up a world of knowledge to students of all abilities and needs. That should include geography and socio-economic status as well as a variety of physical and cognitive needs. Hence good course design should start with thinking about two factors: how students need to access the course, and who will need to access the course.

Creating a community of learners is essential to academic engagement under normal conditions, but it becomes even more critical when there are increased internal and external barriers to accessing and participating in education. However, sometimes those barriers can be overcome with a pedagogical reframing, as we will discuss later in this book. Other times, the problem requires a reframing of the course building process.

CHAPTER 2: DEMOCRATIZING COURSE ACCESS

Accessibility is a complicated and evolving issue, but building your course infrastructure with accessibility in mind can make your learning environment more equitable as well as easier to navigate overall. Course design with an eye on the digital divide as an accessibility problem can help to not only mitigate that gap but also create a more inclusive space overall. The ways a classroom can impact learning are more easily understood in a physical classroom, where lack of ramps or left-handed desks or presence of discussion circles or interpreters are directly observable factors. An online classroom is less direct, but no less important, and the chapter on accessibility provides some tools for building your online classroom. This chapter provides easy to follow instructions about how to create a mobile friendly, accessibility tool friendly, easy to access learning environment.

One exciting part about online teaching and learning is that it puts you and your students in direct contact with the vast amount of information available on the Internet. Creativity is limited only by your imagination and search engine skills. While you are exploring the treasure trove of resources available online, it is important to consider the potential risks of using someone else's copyrighted material. Some of the limitations built into copyright for face-to-face teaching are not available for online courses. One is the Technology, Education and Copyright Harmonization

Act 2002, known as the TEACH Act, which sets the standards for education institutions regarding copyright and specifically addresses online learning. Just as a more global consideration of accessibility is needed in good online course design, a broader vision of what you want to use, how you will use it, and whether copyright allows your use is an important part of the process of course creation.

CHAPTER 3: CONSIDERING COPYRIGHT IN YOUR COURSES

In this chapter an attorney and copyright expert provides a list of questions to walk through when you're considering including a piece of content you didn't create in your online course. It covers topics such as contractual limitations, the public domain, licenses, fair use and permissions. It also provides a brief overview of trademark law with a focus on how you can or cannot use a trademark in your online course. Together, both chapters 2 and 3 will help more of your students get into class and also help you expose them to a wider variety of materials.

In the second part of this book, we will explore how the development of new ways to educate students opens new possibilities to be more inclusive in course design. Enrolling students with different needs means adjustment to work styles, an issue that online learning is uniquely positioned to address. Removing the costs of travel means there are more opportunities to invite speakers to whom students would otherwise not have access. The ability to use libraries and research tools is not diluted by the absence of "brick and mortar" building access. We will show you how to successfully incorporate these tools into your class. The vastness of the Internet means access to new kinds of materials, photos, videos and tools that can fulfill a wider variety of student needs, making online learning enjoyable.

CHAPTER 4: INCLUSIVE COURSE DESIGN

Students from non-dominant cultural groups are systematically less likely to see their individual, community and cultural identities acknowledged, valued or integrated in their day-to-day academic experience. Some states, universities and individual teachers are starting to address these concerns, but the work is only just beginning and must extend beyond any contemporary emergency. Reframing an education system that has underserved diverse students is a long-term goal, but reframing the approach to course design is something that can happen right now, in the LMS in front of you. Here, we show you how to build a class using Universal Course Design, but taking it beyond access to the concept of inclusion and representation. In this chapter, you will learn how to select materials and assignments to create an environment that is reflective of the students who inhabit it.

This chapter will build upon the Community of Inquiry framework and provide examples of how incorporating elements of social, cognitive and teaching presence will allow you to create a more inclusive course structure.

CHAPTER 5: ACCESSIBILITY TOOLS

More than 42 million Americans have some kind of disability, with more than 96% of those conditions being termed "invisible" (Morgan, 2020). This trends with international numbers, which indicate that one in six people have some kind of disability. When it comes to physical conditions, most countries lack the physical facilities or legal frameworks to accommodate people with disabilities (Rafi, 2021). The numbers are telling, people with any kind of disability are half as likely as anyone else to be able to obtain employment. When surveyed about access to advanced degree opportunities, the numbers are even lower. Online learning removes transportation barriers. As mentioned in the first half of this book, design techniques can help remove barriers to accessing online courses and can help overcome Internet access problems. Design can also incorporate features to help the overall learning process for students with certain challenges.

In addition to educational opportunities, every student deserves an engaged, compelling experience. Here we will explore additional tools for these teaching and learning experiences. The goal is to address neurodiversity as well as chronic and physical challenges in ways that create an overall atmosphere of inclusion. Throughout the chapters, we will point out aspects of the class building and design approaches that are either helpful for a variety of students or foster an overall engaged and inclusive community.

CHAPTER 6: MANAGING PACE AND WORKLOAD IN ONLINE COURSES

During the 2020–2021 pandemic in the United States, higher education in many states pivoted online to minimize the spread of COVID-19. Since March 2020, centers for teaching and learning have responded to new challenges to support faculty in planning their online courses. Each semester's challenge has shifted and evolved as faculty adapt to the virtual environment. Multiple questions surfaced as many faculty and students shifted from emergency measures in Spring 2020 to virtual environments for an entire academic year. Persistent questions about balancing asynchronous time and synchronous time existed each semester resulting in multiple discussions about pacing the workload, reimagining assessment options, and developing structures of class time. This chapter provides a snapshot of one center's teaching and learning response to pandemic pedagogy, the existing principles that supported the response, and practical suggestions for teaching and learning to endure in post-pandemic higher education.

CHAPTER 7: APPS, TOOLS AND ASSIGNMENT IDEAS FOR ONLINE ENGAGEMENT

From the awkward transition of taking so-called traditional classroom materials and putting them into a learning management system, to fighting off episodes of the "Zoombies" in your students, teaching online can be a challenge. Finding new ways to engage is beneficial for students, but also for instructors. There are techniques to alter how we think about presentations and depart from overuse of slides. Alternative assignments and assessments not only help with engagement, but offer new ways for students to demonstrate mastery of the material that will not only be more interesting, but create a platform for students that may struggle with traditional testing and writing requirements.

Finally, incorporating a variety of applications and tools into your approach to online teaching and learning is about more than just inclusion and engagement, it harkens to the earlier discussion of pedagogy and our increasingly digital world. The suggested tools and techniques here are inspired by the scholarship of teaching and learning approach, but also consider the concept of digital citizenship and how we and our students can prepare. The hope is that exploring new tools and ways of learning online will inspire an overall flexibility in approach to and acceptance of new ways of receiving information.

CHAPTER 8: DEVELOPING AND INCORPORATING IMPACTFUL LIBRARY RESEARCH GUIDES FOR ONLINE AND HYBRID LEARNERS

Students enrolled in online and hybrid classes tend to be at a relatively high risk of missing out on library resources and services that can help them conduct first-rate research. To address this less-than-optimal situation, librarians, often aided by faculty, develop online library research guides offering curated collections of high-quality, easily accessible library resources and services. This chapter outlines strategies educators can use to enhance the impact of these library research guides for the purposes of inclusive, accessible online learning and research. It focuses on the importance of faculty actively contributing to the creation and dissemination of library research guides, and provides best practices and related checklists to follow when aiming at effective and accessible guide design. Options for library guide incorporation in Learning Management Systems as well as in related course e-materials are also discussed.

Together, this group of writings is meant to help you design a course that is tailored to the online environment, is inclusive and engaging. We will walk you through the course building process with these ideas in mind and offer thoughts meant to challenge the meaning of online pedagogy.

REFERENCES

Blyth, A. (1981). "From individuality to character: The Herbartian Sociology applied to education". *British Journal of Educational Studies*, 29(1), pp. 69–79. Available at: doi:10.2307/3120425. JSTOR 3120425.

Etu, E.-E., Okechukwu, I., Monplaisir, L., & Aguwa, C. (n.d.). "Pandemic disruptions: Virtual learning the new normal for nontraditional students". *ORMS Today*. Available at: https://pubsonline.informs.org/do/10.1287/orms.2020.06.11/full/.

Felten, P. (2013). "Principles of Good Practice in SoTL". *Teaching & Learning Inquiry: The ISSOTL Journal*, 1(1), pp. 121–25. Available at: doi:10.2979/teachlearninqu.1.1.121.

Hendricks, B. (2021, May 17). "What education in the digital economy looks like in America". *TheHill*. Available at: https://thehill.com/blogs/congress-blog/technology/553801-what-education-in-the-digital-economy-looks-like-in-america?rl=1.

Le Pôle. (n.d.). *Home*. History of pedagogy. Available at: https://lepole.education/en/pedagogical-culture/27-history-of-pedagogy.html?showall=1.

Morgan, P. (2020, March 20). "Invisible disabilities: Break down the barriers". *Forbes*. Available at: https://www.forbes.com/sites/paulamorgan/2020/03/20/invisible-disabilities-break-down-the-barriers/?sh=58818b4afa50.

National Student Clearinghouse Research Center. (2021, April 29). "Covid-19: Stay Informed". Available at: https://nscresearchcenter.org/stay-informed/.

Rafi, T. (2021, August 8). "Technology promotes inclusion for the world's largest minority group: People with disabilities". *LSE Business Review*. Available at: https://blogs.lse.ac.uk/businessreview/2021/08/09/technology-promotes-inclusion-for-the-worlds-largest-minority-group-people-with-disabilities/.

Tomei, L. A. (2010). "Designing instruction for the traditional, adult, and distance learner: A new engine for technology-based teaching". *Information Science Reference*.

PART I

Course accessibility and copyright

2. Democratizing course access

Eileen Young

Knowing the challenges some students face just logging on to the
Internet with a good connection, it is easy to imagine the challenges
those same students will face in consistently attending classes online.
There are arguments that the larger Internet should be more accessible
and democratic. In the meantime, how you approach the creation of your
course can make it more democratized.

I   BANDWIDTH

Bandwidth is most easily understood as how much Internet you need
at one time in order to accomplish your goal. Sending an email, for
example, only takes a little bit of Internet, and only when you actually
hit Send, because it's sending some text, once. Streaming video takes up
a lot of the Internet at the same time, because it requires sound and image
constantly. So a synchronous video class takes significantly more bandwidth than a class with only emailed assignments or a discussion board.
This chapter is not advocating for eschewing video calls or synchronous
classroom learning. Rather, it will have some technical descriptions of
what takes up bandwidth and why you should care, along with tools
to allocate bandwidth demands in ways you think are important. Not
everyone has consistent high-speed Internet, due to location or economic
situation, and additionally some are accessing the Internet in ways that
have data caps.

Most frequently when phones are the primary way someone is
accessing the Internet, data caps are a maximum amount of content that
someone can access in a given period. Unless an institution of learning
is providing both mobile hotspots and laptops, consistent access to high
volumes of bandwidth cannot be assumed. It is one of the invisible
barriers that can further marginalize students who are, hypothetically,
using airport Wi-Fi to work on assignments on their way to a funeral, or
evacuated to a hotel with terrible Wi-Fi for the duration of a hurricane, or

living with so many other people that there's never enough bandwidth for everyone to be on a video call when they need to.

There are a couple things that go into how much bandwidth course content takes up. The first is the type of content, as in plaintext versus file uploads. This will be discussed extensively in the "What's in a filetype?" section below. The second is the content of that content; that is, how much non-essential material is included in the content. If you think of the material you're using to teach your students as a package, and bandwidth as the box it's shipped in, part of maximizing accessibility and utility is taking a good hard look at the packing material that takes up space in that box. What's necessary? What makes things easier and is therefore worth the space it takes up?

II   ADD-ONS AND APPS

Apps added to your classroom interface can add a lot of functionality for both you and your students. Part II of this book addresses some of the major highlights and tools, as well as ways to work with your university to maximize utility, so this section will be brief. The major point: opt-in is better than opt-out. "Opt-in" means that tools and ways to adapt content through add-ons and apps are available, preferably in a convenient and easily accessible way, but that students need to take action to make any of those add-ons and apps part of their experience. It also emphasizes that your students are active agents in their own learning and that their consent and engagement both matter.

"Opt-out" means that the add-ons are part of the students' experience from the get-go and they need to turn them off. That means that they need to be using a device that is able to handle those add-ons before they can even access core content. Then they need to be able to identify what the apps are and identify how to turn them off before they can: it's much less user-friendly. This extends even to anti-cheating tools, such as those that lock down the browser or open a second browser.

III   LOCKDOWN BROWSERS

Lockdown browsers are some of the most common anti-cheating tools in a teacher's toolkit outside of plagiarism checkers. They are typically either add-ons or separate programs that monitor or restrict student behavior while taking a test, with features like monitoring faces or not allowing access to websites other than the test-taking page. Having used lockdown browsers as a student, as well as caring about equity, privacy, and computer security, I have developed strong opinions about them. None of those opinions are positive.

For context, I am typing this from my personal laptop, with a phone and iPad next to me, a work laptop in front of me, and a separate work desktop across the room. I am rich in technology: if I were going to cheat, I have a variety of devices that I wouldn't necessarily have to look suspiciously away from my laptop screen to use, making tools that track faces and eye movement prone to errors and completely circumventing blocks on outside websites. Someone less rich in technology wouldn't have that, increasing disparity even amongst "extremely unethical cheating students" as a sample demographic. The system requirements for many of the lockdown tools available also potentially preclude some students from using them at all – for example, many can't be downloaded to a Chromebook. Additionally, lockdown browsers can sometimes disable accessibility add-ons that students may have installed, like those that make text easier to read or disable gifs.

Respondus Lockdown Browser, in particular, also disables function keys – and thus a number of accessibility settings – including but not limited to screen and keyboard backlight brightness. In the event of network interruptions, it also has unpredictable behavior that can completely incapacitate computers due to its refusal to exit or allow alternate windows. If administering an extensive multiple-choice test to a massive introductory level class at a university, it makes some sense to use it, even with all of the above issues. But tests which focus more on critical thinking than searchable facts will frequently be a more effective and equitable tool than the blunt and bloody instrument of a lockdown browser.

IV   SCREENS

The screens students use to access classes cannot be assumed. Some students access the Internet either primarily or only through smartphones, and those have different limitations than a computer monitor. First and foremost: size. A PDF of a book laid out with a single column of text is going to be a frustrating experience to read on a phone. My own phone screen measures 4.7 inches diagonally, and an 8.5 inch x 11 inch page – the standard size when someone uploads a PDF from a scan – measures approximately 14 inches diagonally. That's nearly three times the size of my phone screen, which would mean every line of reading would involve scrolling back and forth across the screen before scrolling down.

This isn't an impenetrable barrier to access, but it's the kind of persistent annoyance that privileged students would not have to face, reinforcing systemic inequities in undesirable ways.

So what's the solution?

The most immediate solution is to not use PDFs.

But that's untenable in other ways; over the course of many years of school, uploaded PDFs have saved me at least thousands of dollars in book fees while giving me access to a wider range of resources and perspectives. Therefore, then, the alternative has to be exploring alternate file types and being judicious in our choices.

V   WHAT'S IN A FILETYPE?

To start: what is a filetype? PDF is a readily recognizable acronym. It stands for Portable Document Format, and the acronym will show up at the end of the filename for a file of this type. There are many file types, though: all it means as an umbrella term is that it is a digital type of file. There are many file types in current use for different purposes, and the ones discussed here are only a small selection of primarily text-focused files, generally referred to by their file extension: the bit that comes after the period at the end of a file name. A good rule of thumb is: if you do not recognize the filetype of a file you encounter, search the Internet for the file extension and "file type" to determine what it is, how you can open it, and whether your students would be reasonably able to open it.

PDF is one of the most used file formats because it is what it says on the tin: a portable document format. It loads and looks the same on every device, pages match so you can actually refer to pages rather than sections, and most scanners can generate them automatically. They're the preferred file type for archiving because they're stable and can be used across platforms. PDFs can also be made to be accessible to a number of specific access needs – Adobe has a guide: https://www.adobe.com/accessibility/pdf/pdf-accessibility-overview.html – but an important part of that is that this form of accessibility is not innate, and has to be ensured and designed in. Usually this design is managed with access to Adobe Pro or an alternative desktop publishing program. Which means that accessible PDFs cannot be generated in a straightforward way from scanned articles, in addition to the issues of file size and fixed page layout.

So what are we looking for in alternatives?

The first is *reflowable text*. That means text that adapts to screen size. It has the downside of largely obviating page numbers, but the upside is that it will be significantly easier to read.

EPUB is a common ebook format, and remixed course content may be available in this format. Creating your own files this way typically requires desktop publishing programs. MOBI is Amazon's ebook format, and any textbook available in the Kindle store is in this format. These work well for the mechanics of reading across different devices and screen sizes, as well as for adjusting for differences in reading preferences and modalities. This extends from the basic accessibility compliance aspect of being accessible to screen readers to more nuanced and minor ways it encourages students to engage. For example, for reading for long stretches, I prefer to get away from the distractions of my computer and read on my phone or tablet, sometimes with Do Not Disturb on. But I don't like to wear my glasses when I'm reading on my phone. If text is reflowable, I can just make the text bigger, and it means that I get fewer, bigger words on the screen rather than having to scroll back and forth. Vision impairment also comes in a wide range, which is why filetype and reflowable text is a matter not just of preference or convenience but access. Because of the complications involved in generating these formats, with both desktop publishing programs and formatting, if a resource isn't already readily available in this format, trying to transform existing resources into this format is not recommended.

DOCX is the format used for Microsoft Word documents. While not necessarily a common format for availability for most articles in journals, it may be available for some archived pre-prints by various authors, and is one you will probably be able to generate easily yourself using most word processing programs. The major advantage of this file format, though, is that the text can be copied from the original file and then pasted directly into your course site. This is a major advantage, because the most accessible filetype is to not upload anything at all. Plain text, with images such as charts available when necessary, is going to be the most accessible to the widest audience. It is inherently reflowable, fitting whatever window it is given, and it requires the least amount of bandwidth to load completely. From the perspective of a student, it is the most accessible format for many.

VI   SCREEN READERS AND IMAGES

This is a term that appears multiple times in this chapter, and deserves some attention independent of other context. A screen reader is a type of software that allows the text on a screen to be read aloud. It also, usually, reads the alt text of any images on the screen – let that be your reminder to use them. It can be understood as an automatically generated audiobook of any given text, with all the same accessibility bonuses and mechanical drawbacks. For an example of this, you can generally have a smartphone or Internet browser read selected text aloud. The voice generally lacks intonation or the natural rhythms of speech, and so isn't necessarily a preferred mode of reading for many people. But it does open access to many students. Not just those with visual impairments, though they are generally the target audience of much screen reading software. Audio availability is also important for students who retain information better that way, for those with long commutes and little time to read otherwise, and generally for students to have more ways to absorb the material. Because screen readers are entirely on the user side, the only important thing to keep in mind is that they read text on a screen (plain text, rich text, or alt text) but not images (like non-optimized PDFs or photos).

Use of images is another important aspect of accessibility. Videos were discussed as an aspect of bandwidth, and that is an important part of the use of images as a class. Images are always more data intensive than text. But the adage that a picture is worth a thousand words persists for a reason, and sometimes images can illustrate a point eloquently. So the trick is to use them when genuinely warranted, and avoid a few items:

- Gifs
  - The movement can be intensely distracting, making them a barrier for some students with neurological differences. For example, with ADHD, it can be very hard to ignore something moving in order to focus on still text.
  - Flashing, particularly bright flashing, can also trigger seizures or migraines. Some students may have add-ons to disable gifs for exactly this reason, but that cannot be assumed.
- Decorative images
  - While fun, they're definitionally unnecessary.
  - If you can be assured of the data access of your students, note that alt text for screen readers on decorative images can just indicate that it's decorative.

VII OTHER FORMATTING

Many people develop preferences for different fonts or other aspects of formatting and design. A colleague, for example, will center-align any column in a spreadsheet that consists entirely of numbers. Is it necessary to the overall function of the spreadsheet? No. But it takes little time and makes them happy, so it persists as a design decision. We all make those design decisions whenever we create something. They are valid decisions that can mesh with teaching style and with the content presented to create a more cohesive whole.

But formatting, too, should be judicious in its application. And setting up defaults that work for you is great, but specifically formatting text on a line-by-line basis or overriding anything the browser itself might try to do is not recommended. For example, coding a paragraph to always show up in a specific font might mean that an add-on to put everything in a dyslexia-friendly font isn't able to present that paragraph in a way a student can read. So minimal intervention in the formatting (in terms of font, alignment, and size) of the text itself is preferred.

A   Curb Cut Effect

The Curb Cut Effect is a concept from public policy, and is based on the idea that adding curb cuts to allow wheelchair users to ascend and descend the curb, such as in parking lots or at crosswalks, also ends up helping people pushing strollers or carts, people with vision impairments, and anyone with mobility issues that impact their ability to step up or down. Designing specifically for one group of people ended up benefitting several other groups as well, like not using GIFs because they can impact people with seizure disorders will also benefit people with very low bandwidth or who get migraines from moving images. Benefits from hitting broad accessibility targets can be extremely broad. That kind of effect is also the goal in making your course content accessible to students; as mentioned in the section on screen readers, they're helpful not just for the direct target audience of the vision impaired but also for those who learn differently or are able to allocate time to listening that they can't to reading. Likewise, many choices you make in intentional design can help students in a wide variety of ways along several different axes.

B   Programming Guide

Generating accessible plaintext from existing material can be fairly simple! With content you're generating yourself or that is in the public domain, it is also straightforward from a copyright perspective. Using items to which you do not own the copyright can be slightly more complicated, though Fair Use in the United States and Fair Dealing in many Commonwealth countries offer significant exemptions for teaching purposes. But this section is not about how to navigate *what* you strip of extraneous formatting and post as plaintext: it's about *how* to do it. The next chapter focuses on copyright and how to navigate it in the context of online learning.

Posting discrete content, like articles or chapters, on their own pages in your course website makes for the easiest navigation in most cases. On Canvas, for example, this lets you easily assign readings to modules and make it easier for students to navigate the course – and for you to track who's even clicked the reading open. But, since the expectation is that you may be using any of several different ways to post a course site, the basic assumptions underlying this guide are that you have: (a) the ability to post content, (b) in either rich text or HTML formats. Most platforms that offer the ability to post in rich text (with formatting such as bold, italics, and links) also have the corresponding ability to edit that text in HTML, though it may be a somewhat obscured option depending on the platform. In many editors, the option is in the top right corner of the box where you can enter text. For specific documentation, you may need to contact your IT department.

You want your readings to have a consistent naming scheme. That means having names for files that follow a pattern that's easy to pick up on. With books, it's easy: the title is on the cover, as is the author's name, and they're generally shelved in a relevant section. The goal is to translate that level of ease of navigation to an online environment. In general, my preference is for page titles that include the author names and article title, but schemes that focus on the due date of the reading, the module it's part of, or the general theme of the reading are all also viable options amongst myriad others. The key to making the readings accessible, though, is consistency; allowing the students to navigate content using a system they can figure out.

Including a link to the original website, journal article, or library page for checking out the book allows for students to read in alternative ways if they prefer, maximizing the ways students can access content.

Table 2.1   *Rich text vs plain text*

Format	Rich Text	Plain Text
Where to paste	Rich text option in text editor	Either rich text or HTML
How to paste	ctrl + v	ctrl + shift + v (in rich text editor) ctrl + v (in html editor)
Benefits	Includes all formatting, such as paragraph breaks, headings, list formatting, etc	Strips all formatting except line breaks
Drawbacks	Extraneous formatting then needs to be stripped	Formatting such as italics, headers, and list formatting then need to be put back in

Including title and author information, if not full citation information, in the body of the page itself also helps encourage good citation habits in students, as well as making it easier for them to reference that information if they want to make notes such as would allow them to cite the reading in a later assignment; page titles aren't always easily visible, especially on smaller screens. But as we start populating the page, there comes the decision point: to copy rich text or plain?

No matter how you paste it, this is now a fairly accessible read, readable on any device and suitable for screen readers and students with limited data. But we can do better!

C   Advanced Programming Guide

This section does not require that you have pre-existing programming knowledge, nor is it, in and of itself, particularly complex. Anyone should be able to follow this guide to code HTML that makes student access to the readings a more streamlined and painless process. This is advanced in that it's the "nice to haves" rather than the "needs" for addressing accessibility. The first step is to make sure you are in the HTML editor of your course page. In many LMS, the option is in the top right corner of the box where you can enter text on a course page. For specific documentation, you may need to contact your IT department. This may then reveal a bunch of hidden formatting, depending on the source you pasted from.

Formatting is important: that's the whole point of this section. But what you omit is as important as what you add. Table 2.2 can be your cheat sheet for most relevant HTML, though additional tools and reference material will be in the Additional Resources section. A good rule of

Table 2.2   *HTML cheat sheet*

HTML	Explanation	When to use
< i >	Italics	As in normal writing
< b >	Bold text	As in normal writing
< H1, h2, etc. >	Headings	As in normal writing, possibly with more frequency in order to ease navigation, and always hierarchical
< cite >	To indicate the title of a cited work	When defining the source of a text quoted
< p >	Defines a paragraph	As in normal writing
< a href>	Defines a link	These can be incredibly useful in online learning, particularly for marking secondary resources. Use as needed
< alt >	The alternative or "hover" text on a link or image	On anything that has more than just text content: images and tables in particular
< style >	Allows changes to the styling of text, including font and color	Never; students may have add-ons on their side to make text more readable, and this might in some circumstances override that while also being bloated code for students on limited bandwidth
< iframe >	Allows embedding of external content	Only when absolutely necessary; links preferred
< embed >	Allows embedding of external content	Only when absolutely necessary; links preferred
< ol >	An ordered (numbered) list	As in normal writing
< ul >	An unordered (bulleted) list	As in normal writing
< li >	An item on a list	As in normal writing; nest within < ol > or < ul > tag
< details >	A collapsible section	For large, discrete chunks of text
< summary >	The portion of a collapsible section that remains visible	For titles or summaries of collapsed sections; nest within < details > tag
< nbsp >	Non-breaking spaces; like a regular space but with 14x the code	Never

thumb is to include only that code which contributes to communicating your message. But HTML in general is fairly lightweight, so a few unnecessary paragraph breaks is not tremendously important: thus its inclusion in the Advanced programming guide rather than the main section.

i   Details

Generally, an article or chapter is going to be a fairly large chunk of text – a pretty intimidating wall of it, for many students. Breaking it into more manageable visual sections makes reading less intimidating and thus hopefully increases engagement with the assigned readings. The primary way we can accomplish this with HTML is by making collapsible sections. This can essentially make a whole reading look initially just like a list of section headers that you click on to read the body of the section. And, excitingly, this doesn't take add-ons or lengthy, complicated programming, and everything is still perfectly readable to a screen reader. There are two main tags you will use to create these sections: <details> and <summary>.

First, before the text you want to collapse, add <details>, then <summary>. Summary is for your section title, or a summary of the text if you don't have section titles. Then you end it using </summary>: the backslash is for an end, a rule that's consistent across HTML. Figure 2.1 has a code excerpt with the HTML tags in lighter text to make them easier to identify.

```
1   <details>
2   <summary>Title or summary goes here</summary>
3   The body of the text goes here;
4   for formatting you might use a <p> tag to define a paragraph.
5   </details>
```

Figure 2.1   Accessibility coding

After the text you want to include in this collapsible section, you end the section with a </details> tag. Congratulations! You have now completed your first collapsible section. The preview in Rich Text won't demonstrate this accurately: by default it will not be collapsed. But if you save the page and then go view it outside of an editing interface, you should see only the text you included inside the summary, accompanied by a plain dark triangle that you can click on to display everything inside the <details> tags.

These sets of tags can be repeated as necessary within a page.

ii   Nesting

For one last option, you can also nest collapsible sections within each other. What does that mean? Say you've copied over the Constitution of the United States because you'd rather your students not have to go to an outside website. You might want to break up the Articles into sections, but then, beyond that, you might also want to have the Sections of each Article also collapse.

The way to format that is to, as before, open a <details> tag, then a <summary> tag for the Article, then close the summary with </summary>. But then, to include the Sections as further levels of collapsible section, do not close the <details> tag. Instead, open another <details> tag, then a <summary> tag for the Section, then close that summary with </summary>. The relevant text for the reading then follows. At the end of that section, you can close it with a </details> tag, then repeat the process for other Sections of the Article. After the last section of the Article, however, you just need to make sure that you have a </details> tag for the Section and another for the Article, which, since this is one layer of nesting, means it should look like </details></details>.

Now for an analogy, since that can be a more comprehensible way to approach things for people who aren't used to thinking about code. Nested sections are like matryoshkas, Russian nesting dolls. They come apart, and have additional dolls inside them. But all of the separate tops, the opening parts, need to match up eventually with the bottom closing parts for it to be a complete matryoshka.

Takeaways from this include:

1. Bandwidth matters.
2. File format matters.
    a.   PDFs are standard but not always accessible.
    b.   Plain text has a lot of advantages.
3. HTML can make plaintext even better, and can be lightweight.
    a.   <details> makes collapsible sections.
    b.   <summary> lets you title those sections.
    c.   </summary> and </details> end your sections.

You have the ability to make your course welcoming and accessible not just through your words and actions but through the online classroom that you create and curate. This chapter has given you some of the digital tools that can help you create an accessible course site; the next chapter will help you navigate part of populating that site by discussing copyright as relates to the academic setting.

3. Considering copyright in your courses

Raven Lanier

Whether you're creating a new online course or moving a face-to-face course online, it's important to think about copyright law. If you use someone else's work in a way that infringes their copyright, you could receive a take down notice and have to remove the work (disrupting the course), you could be required to pay for the use of the work (plus any potential damages), or you and your institution could be sued. Thoughtfully considering copyright law when creating and incorporating content into your course can minimize the chance of any of these disruptions.

This chapter will provide you with a basic, practical understanding of US copyright law by walking you through the questions you should ask every time you want to include a piece of content in your course that you didn't create (referred to in this chapter as "third-party works"). It will also explain the differences between copyright and trademark and will provide a brief overview of how and when you might use a trademark in your course or apply a trademark to something you created.

BOX 3.1   COPYRIGHT IS TERRITORIAL

When thinking about copyright law, it's important to remember that copyright is territorial; it's different in each country. This chapter focuses solely on copyright law in the United States. Users' rights in copyright law (like fair use) are different or non-existent outside of the United States. If you're based out of another country or are teaching learners who are living in a country outside of the United States, you should consider that country's copyright law.

I   HOW CAN I USE A THIRD-PARTY WORK?

When deciding whether or not to include a third-party work in your course, ask yourself the following questions, in order. If the answer to any of them is "yes" you can stop there; your use is likely allowed under copyright law.

1. Is the work in the public domain?
2. Is the use allowed under an existing license?
3. Is your use a fair use?

Before we dive into the three main questions, you should first consider whether your use is allowed by terms of service or the Digital Millennium Copyright Act (DMCA). If the answer is no, stop here; do not work through the rest of the questions.

II   DO THE TERMS OF SERVICE AND DMCA ALLOW YOUR USE?

Depending on where you got the third-party work, there may be restrictions outside of copyright law that affect how you can use the work, especially if you found the work online. These restrictions are commonly found in the website's terms of service (sometimes called "terms of use" or "terms and conditions"). Before including any third-party content from a website, you should read these terms carefully for any restrictions on the way you can use the content.

For example, some terms say that you cannot reproduce content found on the site. If you wanted to take a screenshot of the site to include in your online course, your use would violate the terms of service. Even if your use is allowed under copyright law, the terms of service can stop your use. Ignoring terms of service can lead to consequences, including being banned from the website or sued for breach of contract. If your use is blocked by the terms of service, you can still link to the material, find it on another website (potentially with less restrictive terms), or ask the website for permission to use the work.

If you want to include a third-party work that was originally from a DVD, Blu-Ray, CD, or another format that includes technological protection measures (TPM) that prevent copying, breaking the TPM to copy the work for your online course may be a violation of the DMCA. There are ways to use TPM protected content without breaking the TPMs. For example, you could use screen capture technology to record a scene from a DVD without having to break the TPM to make a copy of the film. If your use would require breaking the TPM, there are DMCA exemptions that allow the breaking of TPM to make copies in some specific circumstances, including some that cover use of a work in an online course. If you are interested in a use that requires breaking a TPM, make sure that your use is allowed by one of these exemptions. Keep in mind that the exemptions are for three years; after three years, exemptions may continue, expand, or even end, and new exemptions may be added. For an updated list of exemptions, see https://www.law.cornell.edu/cfr/text/37/201.40.

BOX 3.2   LINKING VS EMBEDDING

When you link to content online, you provide learners with a URL or hyperlinked text that directs them out to a website. Linking out is a copyright-risk-free way to share content with learners. Since that website (and not a website hosted by or in partnership with your institution) is the one displaying the potentially copyrighted material, only the website takes on the risk of copyright infringement. There are two major cons to linking: (1) the links could break and the content could disappear, and (2) the linked out website may have accessibility issues for students with disabilities.

Embedding is when you mirror content from another website (like a YouTube video, Tweet, or Instagram post) onto your own website or learning management system. Because you or your institution is now publicly displaying the material, you could be liable for copyright infringement. A website making it easy to embed and share does not necessarily mean you can embed and share the material; confirm with the terms of service to see if you're granted a license to embed the work. YouTube's terms of service currently include this license; Instagram's do not (as of 2021). How the courts think about copyright and embedding is currently evolving, so consult a local copyright expert for the most up-to-date information.

More information about how to link and embed content in your LMS can be found in Chapter 2.

III   IS THE WORK IN THE PUBLIC DOMAIN?

Within the realm of copyright, the public domain is an abstract place that holds every work that is not protected by copyright. This includes works that were never copyrightable in the US, works whose copyright has expired (for a variety of reasons), and works whose copyright holders have dedicated them to the public domain. Public domain works can be freely used without any restrictions. If the third-party work you want to use is in the public domain, you can remix it, copy it, sell it; the work is completely free for you to use in any way that you want.

When deciding if a work is in the public domain, first look to see if the work is copyrightable. In order to be protected by copyright, the work must contain some spark of creativity and be fixed in a way that can be repeatedly perceived by a human (including through the help of a machine). It does not protect ideas, facts, procedures, processes, or things like weights and measurements. Copyright also does not protect words or short phrases. If the third-party work falls into any of these categories, it is not protected by copyright. A combination of these uncopyrightable elements may be copyrightable, if the combination is creative enough. For example, an alphabetical list of restaurants in your town would not be copyrightable, but a list of your favorite restaurants likely is (though it would not keep other people from independently listing their own favorites).

There will likely be some instances where you want to use a third-party work (for example, a chart, graph, or other infographic), but you are interested in adapting the work to make it your own. If you take only the idea from the work and not the creative expression, you are not infringing the copyright of the work. To understand the difference between the unprotectable idea and the protectable creative expression, imagine a duck. Now imagine that the duck is wearing sunglasses. What does your duck look like?

It may look like the duck pictured here, or it may look slightly different, depending on your experiences. There are things – like bills, wings, feathers, and leathery webbed feet – that every duck is going to have. Those things you must have in order to draw a duck wearing sunglasses are not protected by copyright. The way that we each imagined our duck, the things that make our ducks distinct from one another, is the creative expression that can be protected by copyright.

Figure 3.1   Duck wearing sunglasses

The idea of a duck wearing sunglasses can be expressed in many ways, but not all ideas can. If the idea can only be expressed in limited ways, they are not protected by copyright. When you are adapting a third-party work, our sunglass wearing, feathered friend will remind you when you are taking the uncopyrightable idea and when you are taking something more.

Works created by a US federal government employee (excluding faculty at certain military academies and institutions, see https://www.law.cornell.edu/uscode/text/17/105 for more information) in the scope of their employment are not covered by copyright and are in the public domain; this means that things like CDC infographics, NASA photographs, and other federal government agency reports are all free to use in any way. Many other works are also in the public domain. If the third-party work was published in the US over 95 years ago, it is in the public domain. Works published in the US before 1989 could be in the public domain for a variety of reasons; if you are interested in using a third-party work that was published before 1989, consult the Copyright Term and the Public Domain in the United States chart (https://copyright.cornell.edu/publicdomain) for detailed information on how to decide if the third-party work is in the public domain. The chart is updated annually and contains the most up to date information about when a work will fall into the public domain.

BOX 3.3   AVOIDING PLAGIARISM

Although copyright law does not require you to provide citations or attributions for public domain works, it is important to follow the citation norms of your field to avoid plagiarizing. Plagiarism can refer to both crediting someone else's work as your own and crediting your work as someone else's. You can avoid plagiarizing by providing an appropriate citation or attribution.

IV   IS THE WORK AVAILABLE UNDER AN EXISTING LICENSE?

In some instances, you may have permission to use a third-party work under an existing license. This could be through an open license (like a Creative Commons (CC) license, see https://creativecommons.org/) or through a license that was purchased by your institution. As long as the license allows your use and you follow the terms of the license, you can include the third-party work in your online course.

CC licenses were created to help copyright holders who want people to be able to use their work, with some limitations, without having to come to the copyright holder for permission. CC licenses are designed to be easy to read and understand, even without a legal background or much knowledge of copyright. They are also machine readable, making it easy for search engines and websites to filter by works that are licensed openly.

There are four CC license options: attribution (BY), sharealike (SA), non-commercial (NC), and no derivatives (ND). The BY license requires attribution back to the original author or copyright holder. The SA license requires that any new works that use the original work are licensed under the same license. The NC license requires that all uses of the work be non-commercial; no commercial uses are allowed. Finally, the ND license does not allow you to remix, transform, or build upon the material.

With the exception of the "no rights reserved" CC0, which waives all copyright in the work and places it in the public domain, all CC licenses require attribution (BY). The other three types of CC license options (SA, NC, ND) can be mixed and matched in a variety of ways to fit the needs of the copyright holder. When looking for works under a CC license, remember that CC BY is the most open license, while CC BY-NC-ND (which allows for non-commercial reproducing and sharing only) is the most restrictive. Symbols are commonly used to show the license that has been applied to the work, examples of which are below.

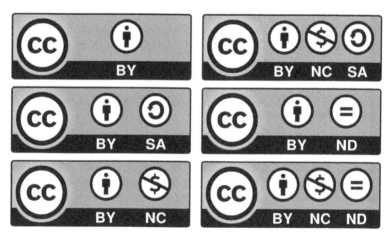

Figure 3.2   Creative Commons licenses

When using a CC licensed work, it is important to include a proper attribution. Attribution best practices advise following the acronym TASL: title, author, source, and license. Each attribution should include the title of the work, the author of the work, a link to the original source, and a link to the license that is applied to the work. Attributions including all four elements of TASL make it easy for others to find the work you are using and know how they can use it in the future. Attributions can be placed anywhere as long as they are reasonably findable and consistent across your online course.

BOX 3.4 APPLYING A CC LICENSE

When you create a new work (for example, an educational resource for your online course), you may want to widely share that work with others. Applying a CC license is an easy way to achieve this goal. CC's License Chooser (https://creativecommons.org/choose/) can help walk you through which license is the best based on your needs and goals.

Some third-party works you want to include in your online course may already be licensed through your institution. For example, your institution's library may subscribe to databases that include journals, newspaper articles, and e-books, all of which are available to your students at no extra cost. To use these resources, you should share the link to the resource in the library's catalogue (or another proxied link) so students can be directed to sign in and view the resource. This allows the library to track how resources are being used so they know to continue to provide them. It also allows the publisher to track uses and accurately share revenue with authors.

V   IS YOUR USE A FAIR USE?

Fair use is a users' right in US copyright law that allows you to make certain uses (including uses that further criticism, commentary, and teaching) without needing permission from the copyright holder. Fair use is very context specific; in fact, there are no bright line rules when it comes to fair use. Everything hinges on what work you are using and the specific ways you want to use it. A fair use analysis is required for each piece of third-party content you want to use under fair use; one analysis likely will not cover all of your uses. Although fair use typically favors teaching and education, not all educational uses will be a fair use.

Each fair use analysis should look at the four fair use factors, which will be covered more in depth. These factors are not a checklist, nor should they be considered in a vacuum. All four factors play off of one another and must be considered together. The four factors are outlined in 17 U.S.C. §108 and are as follows:

1. the purpose and character of the use, including whether such use is of a commercial nature or is for nonprofit educational purposes;
2. the nature of the copyrighted work;
3. the amount and substantiality of the portion used in relation to the copyrighted work as a whole; and
4. the effect of the use upon the potential market for or value of the copyrighted work.

Columbia University has a helpful Fair Use Checklist (https://copyright .columbia.edu/basics/fair-use/fair-use-checklist.html) that lists each issue you should consider when going through the four factor analysis. You can find a copy of the checklist in the appendix.

A   Factor 1 – purpose and character

The first factor looks at the purpose and character of your use, including whether or not your use "transforms" the third-party work. Transformative uses give the third-party work a new purpose – they turn it into something completely different with a new meaning and message – and are more likely to be a fair use under this factor. This factor also takes into account whether your use is commercial or non-profit/educational. Uses that are non-profit/educational are favored under fair use, but commercial uses can also be fair, especially if the use is transformative.

B   Factor 2 – nature of the copyrighted work

The second factor looks at the nature of the third-party work, meaning whether it is factual or creative. If you are using a more factual work, this weighs in favor of fair use. Use of a more creative work (e.g., a work of fiction) weighs against fair use. Finally, this factor takes into consideration whether the third-party work is published or unpublished; if the work is unpublished, this can weigh against fair use.

C   Factor 3 – amount of third-party work used

The third factor looks at how much of the third-party work you want to use when it comes to both quality and quantity. It is commonly believed that as long as you use less than 10% of a work, your use is a fair use. This is a myth. Generally speaking, the less you use, the more likely it is a fair use. However, some uses include 100% of a work and are "still a fair use"; others use less than 10% and are not a fair use. You should use the amount of the third-party work that you need to use in order to achieve your legitimate purpose and no more. The specific amount will depend on the context of your use. This factor also looks at whether the part of the third-party work you want to use is the most important part, or the heart, of the work. If you use the most important part of the work, your use is less likely to be a fair use. This factor hinges on how transformative your use is; the more transformative, the more you will be able to use under the third factor.

D   Factor 4 – effect on the market

The final factor looks at the effect your use of the third-party work has on the market or potential market for that work. For example, if your use would displace the third-party work on the market – if people would stop purchasing the third-party work because they could buy it from you more cheaply or get it from you for free – that greatly disfavors fair use. Similarly, if your use would destroy an established (or could be established) licensing market, that weighs against fair use. This is where the transformative part of factor one comes back into play; if your use is truly transformative, it will be different enough from the original to not compete on the market. If your use negatively impacts the market of the work because of criticism or commentary, that does not weigh against fair use.

VI   ASKING FOR PERMISSION

If you have answered "no" to all four of the above questions, you will need permission from the copyright holder to include the third-party work in your online course. The copyright holder may be the author, the publisher, the author's heir (if the author is deceased), or some other third-party. When asking for permission, make sure that you are clear about how you want to use the work, how long you want to use it, and how many people will view or interact with the work. This will help the copyright holder make an informed decision about whether or not they want to give you permission and how much they want to charge you. Share your deadline with the copyright holder and give them plenty of time to respond; some permission processes can take several weeks, or even months. The copyright holder may have an existing permission form that you can fill out; for other instances, see the example permission form in the appendix.

If you want to be the only one who is able to use the third-party work, you should ask the copyright holder for an exclusive license, and that license must be in writing. If you are fine with others also being able to use the third-party work, you should ask the copyright holder for a non-exclusive license. A non-exclusive license does not have to be in writing, but getting the terms in writing can help if you need proof of the license or need to refer to the terms later.

If you are unable to find the copyright holder, do not get a reply, or are told "no", you may want to reconsider your fair use analysis or consider an alternative for the third-party work. If the third-party work is available on the open Internet, one option is to link students out to that website. A work is considered to be on the open Internet when anyone with Internet access can view the work without hitting a paywall, incurring a charge, or having to create an account. You can link to any content on the open Internet without infringing copyright, but be aware that some websites are blocked outside the US. Students in those countries may not be able to access the content without using a virtual private network (VPN), and they could face legal consequences for using a VPN to access the content. You may also consider replacing the third-party work with one you created or one that is openly licensed under a CC license. Remember, any underlying ideas or facts of a work are free for you to use.

VII   COPYRIGHT VS TRADEMARK

Copyright law promotes the growth of science, art and culture by protecting original, creative expression and sometimes allowing that expression to be used and built upon by others. Trademark law focuses on protecting consumers who are purchasing goods or services by helping them identify the source or brand. It also provides brands and companies with legal protection against counterfeiting and fraud (What is a Trademark? USPTO 2021). While copyright does not protect words and short phrases, trademark law can; it can also protect things like colors, scents, and sounds.

Trademark law does not prevent you from using those words, short phrases, colors, and sounds in your online course as long as you are not using the trademarks in a way that competes with the original on the market or makes it seem like the brand is endorsing or affiliated with your online course. So if you want to talk about, as an example, Apple's business model or Ford's mission statement in your online course, you can show the logos and say or show the brand names without fear of infringing on the companies' trademarks. More information about trademark law, including how to register a trademark and how and when to use the TM, SM, and ® symbols, can be found on the US Patent and Trademark Office (USPTO) website (https://www.uspto.gov/trademarks/basics/what-trademark).

BOX 3.5 TRADEMARKING A PRODUCT OR SERVICE

If you create a new product or service, you may want to trademark that product or service's name, slogan, or packaging. Unlike copyright protection, which applies automatically, you have to register your trademark with USPTO to get federal protection. To register, you have to provide proof of your use of the trademark in the market and pay a fee. If you are interested in registering a trademark, you should reach out to a local attorney for assistance in searching the trademark database and working with USPTO.

VIII CONCLUSION

Copyright can be intimidating (especially for people who have never considered it before) but it doesn't have to be. With the proper tools, all of which have been shared in this chapter, anyone can make good-faith, legal-based decisions about using the content of others in their online course.

PART II

The teaching and learning experience

4.   Inclusive course design

LiAnne Brown

I   INTRODUCTION

As the ways in which institutions of higher education recruit and interact with students diversify, so do the classrooms which these students
inhabit. Beyond being online, in hybrid or flex class environments, the
students themselves are a mix of ethnic, racial and age groups. More non-
traditional or adult learners are choosing an online education. This means
they are navigating the competing demands of work and family alongside
the rigors of pursuing a graduate degree. According to research from
EducationData.org, people seeking graduate degrees are 18.8% more
likely to enroll for those degrees online than undergraduate students. Of
all online learners, about 20% report being from a diverse racial or ethnic
background.

Additionally, the statistics show these learners have more diversity than
just the adult learner experience. The intersections of those experiences,
as illustrated in Figure 4.1, will influence their online engagement. As we
transition from the initial part of this book which examined accessibility
and the growing world of materials available to students online into the
teaching and learning experience, it is important to think about students'
needs as they relate to their overall human experience. Below, in Figure
4.2, we revisit Maslow's hierarchy of needs. Consider those in terms
of the Scholarship of Teaching and Learning, which makes the student
a partner in their learning experience. In this context, we must appropriately partner with and prepare our students by creating a physically or
virtually accessible space that encourages self-actualization.

An important part of this process to self-actualization is about creating
safe spaces where students feel represented and included. This chapter
will present an evidence-based and culturally competent approach to
designing an inclusive online learning environment. Each section will
first present research and data, followed by suggested course design

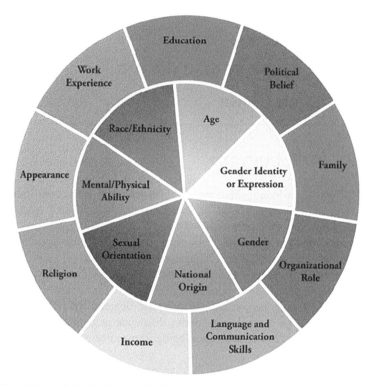

Note: Alt-text: Colorful wheel graphic illustrates primary and secondary dimensions of human diversity.

Figure 4.1   *"Diversity Wheel as used at Johns Hopkins University" is licensed under Creative Commons Attribution 4.0 International*

strategies. As you go through this chapter, we encourage you to refer back to Figure 4.1 and consider these critical factors for content representations in your courses.

II   WHAT WE KNOW ABOUT INCLUSIVE ONLINE LEARNING ENVIRONMENTS

Research and experience tell us that human beings are social learners. Students learn more deeply and effectively if they can create meaningful

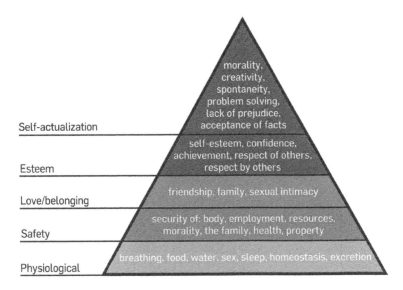

Self-actualization

Esteem

Love/belonging

Safety

Physiological

Note: Maslow's Hierarchy of Needs is licensed under Creative Commons
Attributions-Share-Alike3.0 Unported License.

Figure 4.2   *Graphic representation of Maslow's Hierarchy of
Needs*

connections between their lives and the course content, their fellow classmates, and their instructor. Educators teaching online courses may create
and design more inclusive learning environments through the imple-
mentation of the well-known Community of Inquiry (CoI) Framework.
This framework theorizes that "in-depth and significant learning in
online learning settings depends on the development of a community of
inquiry". The Community of Inquiry Venn Diagram, as shown in Figure
4.3, converges the three domains of engagement with participants, interactions via learning goals/direction, and interaction via learning goals
and direction. This convergence produces a collaborative and inclusive
education experience that includes supportive discourse, an inclusive
learning climate, and regulated learning.

As shown, there are three aspects to CoI: social presence, cognitive
presence, and teaching presence. Researchers like Anderson (2017)
noted that this framework does not adequately account for the fact that
effective teaching is equally dependent upon the learners' experiences in

the classroom. Account for this as you consider the strategies presented in this chapter and consider how to integrate your learners' experiences into the inclusive teaching strategies you choose to employ. This section will further discuss each of the three components of this framework along with examples for how to integrate them into your course design and teaching strategies.

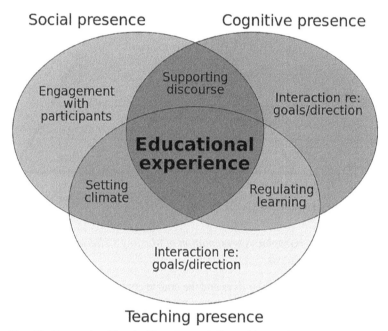

Note: The Community of Inquiry Venn diagram is licensed by Creative Commons CC-by-SA-3.0

Figure 4.3   The Community of Inquiry Venn Diagram

III   SOCIAL PRESENCE

Social presence enables students to feel comfortable online with each other and their instructor. Just as with any relationship building activity, developing and sustaining social presence must be initiated early in your course and sustained throughout. It is important to recognize that most students may bring "baggage" from prior educational experiences into your virtual learning environment. Perhaps a student had a negative experience in their formative or even other higher education experiences concerning an area(s) of disciplinary study such as English composition, a foreign language study, mathematics, or macroeconomics. Or maybe life's challenges have become nearly insurmountable for students who are balancing multiple priorities, personal, or health challenges (career, family, physical and/or mental illness, economic struggle). Such students may enter the online environment with fear, anxiety, uncertainty, and intimidation.

In a cultural and social diversity context, consider the unique needs, challenges and prior experiences of your learning audience and the types of engagement that will promote comfort, safety, and a sense of belonging. Perhaps a student was made to feel undervalued, shamed, embarrassed, or treated with contempt due to a language barrier, vocal accent, or ethnic background. Or perhaps they faced a cognitive, hearing, or vision impairment that was inadequately accommodated, leaving them feeling isolated and excluded from the learning experience. Application of the CoI framework helps to promote quality social engagement and a sense of belonging in the learning environment. Consider creating opportunities for your students to connect with other students' experiences by sharing their prior positive and negative experiences. You may even partner with students to construct a student contract that represents the types of behaviours that will promote inclusion and the cultivation of shared social experiences.

Holding students accountable for their learning and setting clear expectations for the course delivery, feedback, grading, and rules concerning the timely submission of course work is extremely important to effective course management. While you set clear and detailed course expectations for student performance, consider the CoI model and create space to both acknowledge and honor the many challenges your students may face while engaging in your course. Prepare a strategy for how to balance holding your students accountable with reasonable allowances for unforeseen challenges that may impact their ability to participate and meet course expectations. Unnecessarily rigid course expectations may discourage rather than promote an inclusive learning climate.

Creating opportunities to build social presence in your virtual learning environment will create a richer, more meaningful learning experience for your students. Both live and recorded video technology is a great tool to consider. For example, use video snippets to share feedback with students rather than purely text to promote a sense of your presence as their instructor. Jones-Roberts (2018) cited research in which students are "three times more likely to make alterations to assignments which had audio feedback". She also noted research related to discussion forums that indicate that student-to-student video discussions yield "higher self-reported perceptions of social presence". While creating these innovative opportunities, plan for how to accommodate students with cognitive, vision, or hearing impairments to ensure your entire learning audience can actively participate.

Points of reflection to consider as you plan and design your course may include any of the following:

- How do my faculty expectations and course management strategies promote both student accountability *and* social presence?
- How can I create opportunities in discussions and assignments for students to learn through social connection?
- What design and teaching strategies can I incorporate into my course delivery that will promote student social connection?

One way to approach a course design strategy is when creating your syllabus, faculty and student introductions and discussion posts. Use language that will promote social presence. Consider the following verbal cues:

- Verbally convey your authenticity: "I'm glad you're here and I am genuinely interested in your perspective on these topics."
- Draw students into active, participative learning: "While I am your instructor, consider me more of a facilitator that will partner with and guide you in your learning this semester."
- Encourage students to address difficult topics directly, openly and honestly: "The topics we are going to discuss this week may be interpreted as divisive or difficult, particularly for those who may have shared experiences. Let us agree to speak our truth using words that convey respect, empathy and consideration."
- Invite students to build social connection and understanding: "When providing discussion feedback, consider how your experiences are similar to or different than those of your course mates."
- Provide opportunities for real-world application of course topics: "Share an example out of your lived experiences, personally or professionally, that relates to this topic. How do the readings compare/ contrast with your experience? How do you interpret your lived

experience as a result of the course readings or interactions with course mates?"
• Leverage LMS resources that promote social presence such as student profiles. Encourage students to view each others' profiles to seek opportunities to build social connections.

Set clear expectations regarding your availability to your students to connect with them outside of the learning environment during your office hours. Consider building a **social presence dashboard** (you could use MS Word, Excel, or a GoogleDoc to capture the information) on which you capture how to connect with your learning audience based on information that each has shared with you. While this may not always be possible when teaching 200 students, it may certainly be possible with smaller class sizes of 30 or fewer students or by utilizing information provided on student-created profile pages. Students appreciate when instructors recall information they have shared, and/or use that information as part of classroom engagement and will be much more likely to engage in their coursework with classmates and their instructor.

Consider incorporating these five strategies for increasing social presence into your online learning environment, as introduced by Jones-Roberts (2018):

1. Use scaffolded, self-reflective topics to break the ice, such as:
   a. Introductory posts that encourage storytelling and allow students to speak about both their strengths and challenges.
   b. Breakout discussions (both live and asynchronous) to pair students to interact and share something about one another with the group.
   c. Introductions that allow students to share their cultural experiences, whether ethnic or socio-cultural experiences.
   d. Lighthearted topics that reduce nervous tension by discussing a favorite childhood memory, family tradition, favorite season, food, or physical location in which they feel most at peace.
   e. Use of typology assessments, such as MBTI, color personality test, or Gallup StrengthsFinder. Sharing the results from these assessments will create opportunities for building social connections and promoting a deeper understanding and appreciation of fellow course mates.

2. Encourage personal reflection and disclosure to provide reasons for engaging further beyond academic achievement or meeting minimum participation requirements. Examples include:

    a. Encourage students to share what they enjoyed the most or least about a particular weekly activity and why.

    b   Encourage students to reflect on a concept they disagreed with.

    c. Encourage students to reflect on how concepts covered have challenged their prior knowledge or perspective and how their assumptions or perceptions may be changed as a result.

    d. Encourage students to share how they will apply their learning to personal and/or professional practices, and what will motivate them to continue to use that newly acquired knowledge (for increased knowledge retention).

    e. Depending on the nature of our course content, encourage students to consider how known or hidden biases may serve as a barrier to their effective learning and building social connections with their fellow learners. Consider providing free resources for taking hidden bias assessments that also provide meaningful feedback on how to interpret the results and use them to work towards developing self-awareness, emotional intelligence, and cultural competence.

3. Create media pieces, such as short videos, to introduce or close out each week of learning.

    a. Seeing your face and hearing your voice and authentic expression will allow students the opportunity to connect emotionally with you as an instructor. Use authentic language to express what you hope they have learned and why, applauding their efforts and calling out any areas that are opportunities for improvement and growth.

    b. Encourage students to create a video as an option for discussion postings or other types of assignments, especially if discussions are asynchronous.

4. Use video conferencing or other team call software available for live classroom lecture and discussion. Ensure that your video content also includes a transcript and closed captioning for students using assistive technology. Set expectations for students to be on camera, and create opportunities for both course related interaction as well as personal interaction (such as sharing a pet, children, or a favorite item in their study space). To better accommodate students with vision impairment, encourage students to state their name when speaking.

Depending on what is available or authorized for use at your institution, video conferencing platforms include:

a. Adobe Connect.
b. Webex.
c. Google Chat.
d. Zoom.
e. Zoho meetings.
f. RingCentral.
g. Microsoft Teams.
h. BigMarker.
i. Kaltura.
j. Blackboard Collaborate.
k. GotoMeeting.
l. Blue Jeans.

5. Provide audio feedback directly to students on assignment and discussion submissions, or collectively to the entire class during collaboration sessions or in the discussion board.

Other social presence suggestions include:

- Provide encouragement that promotes self-efficacy through positive reinforcement.
- Draw in learners to participate using inclusive words like *we, us, you, and all* and provide an opportunity for students to identify their preferred personal pronouns for gender identification.
- Provide compliments with the goal of praising, validating, and drawing students into the learning community.
- Provide compliments that set up more instructive statements.
- Offer social information that encourages engagement in the learning community.
- Share personal experiences and encourage students to share their lived experiences to build consensus, cultural understanding and social connection.

(Granite State College, n.d.)

IV   COGNITIVE PRESENCE

Cognitive presence describes an instructor's ability to stimulate students to grow from where they are to where the course is designed to take them. Sezgin's research on cognitive presence (2021) indicates that "cognitive presence is possible only when individual variety exists in online settings". Consider how you can engage your learning audience on their journey to meeting course learning goals. Creating learning events that trigger thought (a triggering event) can lead to increasing depth in practical learning, including exploration (such as brainstorming, offering fellow students' suggestions or exchanging information), integration (synthesizing information such as essay or group presentations), or achieve resolutions (such as engagement in research or case studies that require a student to apply theoretical perspectives, test, and defend findings) (Sezgin, 2021). The incorporation of a variety of different engagement strategies that encourage interaction and social learning will improve the degree of cognitive presence in your virtual classroom.

Planning a variety of formative assessment methods into your course delivery is key to increasing cognitive presence. Key findings from a 2014 Hanover Research study indicate that while there are varying opinions on the effectiveness of different formative assessment tools, students who receive formative assessment **perform better on a variety of performance indicators than their peers**. Formative assessment as a means for increasing cognitive presence involves five aspects, according to the Black and Wiliam 2009 framework:

- Clarifying learning intentions and criteria for success.
- Engineering effective classroom instruction and other learning tasks that elicit evidence of student understanding.
- Providing feedback that moves learners forward.
- Activating students as instructional resources for one another.
- Activating students as the owners of their learning (self-efficacy).

Ensuring that your learning audience has a clear picture of their current state, prior knowledge of the subject matter, and intended future state is an important aspect of creating and sustaining cognitive presence in your virtual learning environment. Pre- and post-assessment of learning and general Q & A discussion forums allow for opportunities to provide meaningful feedback to students both individually and collectively on their understanding, retention, and ability to build new learning connections based on what has been covered.

Creating opportunities for students to serve as instructional resources for each other is a great way to build cognitive and social presence in your online learning environment. Students' prior life and learning experiences may be leveraged for the enrichment of their fellow learners. Particularly for students who might not otherwise be inclined to participate, the opportunity to provide and receive peer review may produce positive results that break down barriers of apprehension and fear of interaction in the online learning environment. Activities such as peer review, learner-led course activities like a laboratory activity, or learner-facilitated discussions are key formative activities that promote student inclusion through cognitive presence.

Points of reflection to consider to build cognitive presence in your online learning environment may include any of the following:

- How can I be more intentional about creating learning trigger events that draw my learners into the course content?
- What types of formative activities have I planned for my students to measure learning beyond assignments and discussions?
- How am I creating inclusive self-assessment opportunities for students to increase their sense of self-efficacy in their learning?
- What opportunities can I create for my students to serve as instructional resources for each other? What guidance should I provide as criteria for success?

There are a variety of course design and delivery strategies that can be employed to increase cognitive presence in an online learning environment, including either of the following:

- Clear rubrics with detailed descriptors for at least five progressive domains of performance and provide inclusive language.
- Providing clear, specific and detailed formative feedback on how to improve.

Explore these online cognitive strategies as outlined by the University of Virginia Center for Teaching Excellence. As you do, consider the diversity of your learning audience and how these cognitive presence strategies can be utilized to also build and sustain social connections between students. Call out difficult discussions or reflection. Ensure the variety of assignments reflect diversity of thought, social, and ethnic lived experiences.

V   TEACHING PRESENCE

Teaching presence is the instructor's ability to engage in course planning and guide the online course delivery so that teaching goals will be met

Table 4.1   Activity structures

Start with the end in mind and clearly communicate what students will learn in class.	Provide a variety of assignments that students can pick and choose from to demonstrate learning.	Provide a variety of different types of content and assignments: video, writing, audio, reflection, team-based work, readings, games, etc.	Provide many low-stakes formative assessment opportunities.	Encourage reflection.
Design discussion prompts and dive deep into engaged discussions.	Use role playing activities to illustrate multiple points.	Have students lead discussions.	Develop group work where students work as teams.	Provide peer-review opportunities with clear rubrics for assessment.
Connect current learning content to previous content/ learning.	Have students reflect on what they are learning now and how they will use this knowledge in the future.	Encourage multiple perspectives and dialogue to understand those perspectives.	Model and support diverse points of view in online discussions.	Provide opportunities for group brainstorming, such as designing concept maps together.
Provide opportunities for insight on how others are thinking through tools such as polling, breakout rooms, or team assignments.	Develop grading rubrics that clearly indicate the quality of different answers and the corresponding scoring.	Post examples of completed assignments.	Have students create or find relevant materials and post them to the class as resources.	Provide frequent opportunities for feedback and testing.

(Ward Oda et al., n.d.). As indicated in the CoI model, inclusive learning environments collaboratively apply cognitive and social presence elements along with effective teaching strategies that promote meaningful learning. A 2010 research study that examined online teaching presence and how it relates to student success outlined three factors of teaching presence: instructional design and organization (layout and structure that promotes active interaction with the instructor), facilitation of discourse (i.e., discussion feedback that promotes follow up questions and critical thinking), and direct instruction (providing substantive explanatory feedback during discussions and during assignment grading).

Students surveyed on which teaching presence factor had the greatest impact on their success reported facilitation (45%) as the most important factor, followed by direct instruction (44%). Conversely, when surveyed on which teaching presence factor had the greatest impact on their failure, those surveyed indicated instructional design and organization (45%) as the most impactful factor, followed by direct instruction (34%). Poor course design and organization leads to confusion and challenges with students' ability to track their progress and attainment of stated learning outcomes. Content organization and clear communication of instructions for each week are critical to student success. Most learning management systems provide structural elements that allow you to arrange course content in an easy-to-follow sequence along with visual cues like images or graphics. As noted in the section on cognitive presence, starting out each week with setting clear expectations for what students will learn helps provide content structure and organization. Ensure that all learning resources are grouped in the same section and are easy to locate. Establish and follow a similar structure to discussion board questions so students know what to expect, in general. While you may wish to change up the types of media and engagement involved, the structural design should be clear, concise, and easy to follow.

Establish a clear rubric that outlines expectations related to discussion posts as well as responses to other learners. If you choose to plan for break out sessions or learner-facilitated discussions, ensure that students are aware of these specialized discussion formats. Provide clear and easy to follow instructions along with a rubric that defines expectations for performance and participation. Keep content simple the first time to give students a chance to gain comfort with accessing break out rooms and working through instructions. Create sample posts or assignments to provide clarity so students know how their course work should be structured along with the level of detail expected.

A   Content Chunking

Online course content should provide a blend of readings, media, and other interactions that will build and reinforce learning. Check each of your weekly course sections to ensure they are structurally similar and easy to follow. Keep track of the amount of time on task expected each week. If a particular week(s) will entail more time on task than other weeks, ensure you inform students so they can plan for that additional time in their schedules. Consider how many readings and/or activities are expected of students from one week to the next and ensure they are reasonable in scope for the course content and number of credit hours. These considerations promote inclusive learning, allow students to work the course time commitment into their other life priorities, and avoid feeling overwhelmed or falling behind. Encourage students to reach out if they are struggling with heavy coursework loads to make assignment submission arrangements as needed and as your time and schedule will allow.

B   Teaching Presence in Direct Instruction

In addition to design elements, teaching presence also relates to how effectively you interact with and provide explanatory guidance for your students as they progress through their course work. Inclusive teaching presence involves the use of techniques that "pull together student ideas, provide resources, share ideas, inject elaboration, provide technical assistance, and build learning connections" (Granite State College, n.d.). As noted in previous sections, seek opportunities in your teaching strategies to consider the unique needs of a socially and/or ethnically diverse learning audience. Ensure that course materials reflect clear language and relatable examples that can be understood by a socially and culturally diverse audience, including those who are non-native English speakers and/or are part of the LGBTQ+ community.

Some reflective points to consider include any of the following:

- Are my weekly course materials organized in a way that is predictable, organized, and easy to follow?
- Do expectations and the course outline in my syllabus follow the content in the course?
- Is the amount of instructional material reasonable for the course depth and semester hours? Might course work overwhelm my audience and discourage robust participation?
- Have I provided adequate instructions for all course activities? What activities might confuse students, for which I may need to provide additional instructions or examples?
- Do students know how to contact me with issues? Have I provided an expectation of how soon I will respond to their inquiries?

Consider the following strategies for promoting and sustaining teaching presence in your courses:

- Consider a clear and easy to follow modular course structure:
  - Build out one full week, then copy that structure into subsequent weeks to provide consistency in both structure and the sequencing of course content.
  - Outline clear expectations for student learning through the use of grading rubric.
    - Use inclusive language that encourages learner participation.
- Balance time on task each week to ensure learners don't get overwhelmed by course work:
  - Set clear expectations concerning how much time on task students should expect each week.
  - If a week happens to be content heavy or will utilize formative methods that are unique or require special instructions or preparation, provide that information to students in advance so they can plan for that additional or unique engagement.
  - Ensure the amount of course work is reasonable for the course level and number of semester hours.
- Maintain presence in your course by setting expectations on when you will perform grading, provide feedback, and encourage live interaction via office hours for video or phone calls.

Consider using any of the following teaching prompts that reflect strong teaching presence:

- Pulling together: summarizing or pulling together a student's or multiple students' ideas.
- Providing resources: adding information or details to a discussion.
- Sharing ideas: directing students to provide more information by sharing with them your thoughts.
- Teaching elaboration: expanding on an idea to make a point. Goes beyond confirmation of the student response and typically uses an example to illustrate the point.
- Making social connections: deepening understanding by making connections between new knowledge and established understandings, experiences, or knowledge. (Granite State College, n.d.)

VI   UNIVERSAL COURSE DESIGN (UDL) FRAMEWORK

Universal Design for Learning or Universal Course Design is a framework designed to both improve and optimize the teaching and learning experience by structuring learning in a way most consistent with how the human brain builds learning connections. The UDL model supports inclusive learning in its three primary elements (UDL, n.d.):

* Providing multiple means of engagement.
* Providing multiple means of representation.
* Providing multiple means of action and expression.

The goal is to create learners who are motivated, knowledgeable and goal-oriented, among other things. The path to successfully using UDL is one in which the instructor shifts their thinking about how a broad learning audience learns. Rather than a prescriptive methodology, it is a means of translating theories into practical applications. It is flexible, expanding beyond teaching theory and application to the teaching of various theories and helping a range of learners apply them consistently. UDL complements student-centered pedagogy in that the student is included in and sometimes is a co-creator of the learning process.

UDL is also known as an approach that seeks to meet the needs of all learners while meeting the needs of those with specific challenges. It is a way to expand our practical applications of teaching and learning to ensure no students are left to the margins. It can also be an approach to specific aspects of marginalization in education. Later in this section, we will discuss some of those specifics, especially ones concerning accessibility and accommodation. Here, we focus on how this design approach can be used to promote inclusive learning.

Creating an inclusive classroom is firstly an issue of climate. If done improperly, "Classroom climate is affected not only by blatant instances of inequality directed towards a person or group of people, but also by smaller, more subtle 'micro-inequities' that can accumulate and have significant negative impacts on learning" (Hall, 1982). Instead, the climate can be one of inclusion and representation to draw in an audience with varying learning abilities, lived experiences, and social backgrounds. Some of the ways to create an inclusive classroom climate include being self-reflective. Just as you consider how students' backgrounds and experiences could manifest themselves in the classroom, you should consider your own life experiences. Consider how to leverage your experiences as a positive force in the classroom. Think through how your social or cultural bound assumptions could play a part in your teaching or cognitive presence. Then seek out information, tools, and resources that will help you correct any inaccurate assumptions that could impact your classroom climate and course delivery. Set ground rules for the classroom climate ahead of time and address any incivilities as they arise. Also acknowledge your vulnerability and check in on the classroom climate periodically.

VII   INCREASING RACIAL AWARENESS AS A MEANS OF INCLUSIVE TEACHING

Promoting social and cognitive presence requires an awareness and attentiveness to the unique needs of your learning audience. Preparing to teach a diverse online audience requires an awareness of the concerns, challenges, and needs of students from different ethnic and social backgrounds. Social psychologist Maja Becker conducted a global survey to learn about how culture impacts self-esteem in learning environments. She found that the self-esteem concept is often tied to the norms of the dominant culture, and students overvalued the achievement of those priorities articulated by the dominant culture (Becker et al., 2014). As the division between students' own culture and dominant priorities broadened, there was an inverse relationship with self-esteem as it is tied to the educational environment.

Faculty appointments at institutions of higher education often reflect the lack of diverse representation needed for inclusive learning environments. This is underscored by data from the National Center for Education Statistics, which shows that Latinx, Afro-descendants and multi-racial individuals are underrepresented amongst tenure track roles in higher education. Native Americans have no representation in those roles. Moreover, the experiences and numerical representation of LGBTQ+ faculty are not consistently tracked in university diversity programs. These hiring trends are out of sync with the growing number of students from these groups enrolling in undergraduate and graduate programs (Matias, 2021). For the online classroom, closing this representational gap means bringing a level of intentionality to creating a civil, bias-avoidant environment.

A group of researchers from Brookings specifically studied discrimination in online classrooms. They questioned whether traditional classrooms, where gender and racial bias was heavily present, would impact student performance (Baker et al., 2018). What they found was a racial bias in both instructor and student interactions. They intentionally used an online discussion board as their framework, because it is a more anonymized setting than a virtual classroom, with faces in full view of the person teaching. Even in this environment, these researchers noted that posts from white male students received twice the instructor responses as other groups. While they did not correlate the bias to lower classroom performance, this researcher provides an important cautionary context for all those teaching in online environments. Another study noted that students are more likely to respond to the posts of those who are in their same representational groups, such as gender or race (Jaschik, 2018). Hence, in an online course where there is low representation of individuals of a particular race or ethnic background, a less equitable level of interaction and inclusion could likely result.

Scholar Cathy Davidson wrote specifically to the experiences of students throughout the COVID-19 pandemic period, noting that "our students are learning from a place of dislocation, anxiety, uncertainty, awareness of social injustice, anger, and trauma" (Humphrey & Davis, 2021). These realities are only further exacerbated by the social injustices experienced more acutely by members of the LGBTQ+, ethnic minorities, individuals with disabilities, and other marginalized groups. Promoting more inclusive learning environments means acknowledging and examining these issues with your students and seeking meaningful connection points between their lived cultural experiences and course subject matter.

In your course design it is important to be intentional about your approach to different topics. Acknowledge that there are a variety of opinions and perspectives in society and seek out resources, such as course materials and any guest speakers, that represent diverse social, ethnic, and gender-based perspectives. Students should feel free to express diverse opinions as part of a culture that pursues knowledge from a variety of sources. When the topic is addressing race, gender or ethnic issues it is important to decentralize the values of the dominant culture and instead assign equal value to a variety of cultural perspectives. That can range from removing maleness as the standard for measuring the human experience and allowing other genders and cultural identities to predominate in the materials presented to students. Following our examination of course design that is driven by theory into practice and research indicating the harms of bias; our next step is to take into practice what we have surmised in public and professional discourse: representation matters.

VIII DIVERSE REPRESENTATION IN COURSE CONTENT DESIGN

Previous sections discussed how to build social and cognitive presence in your courses by considering the unique needs of a diverse learning audience. Accomplishing this goal requires you to create opportunities to connect with your learning audience through the measures you employ for creating strong social, cognitive, and teaching presence. Course design with diverse representation entails course planning with a diversity mindset such as seeking learning resources authored by individuals who reflect diversity of thought and lived experiences. Course readings, publications, media such as videos, photos or graphics should be considered through a diversity lens.

Points of reflection may include any of the following:

- Can my students see themselves or others who look like them in the course materials I have provided?
- Do the case studies or other media I have provided include a diversity of thought and background such as ethnicity, age, and gender identification, or a physical, mental, or cognitive disability? Could all members of my learning audience connect to some aspect of my course materials? Have my course materials alienated a segment of my learning audience?
- Have I ensured that my course materials are accessible and meet the needs of learners requiring cognitive, hearing, or vision accommodations?
- Have I actively acknowledged when course materials (reading or media) inadequately represent the history or experiences of a particular group represented in my learning audience or disproportionately represent the view/lived experiences of one group?
- Do course content examples reflect the lifestyle norms of a variety of socio-economic groups?

One of the most straightforward course design strategies you can take is to diversify your examples. Consider providing examples that are outside of your lived experiences. Those can be using names, situations, images, background music, and other media forms that represent wide social and cultural experiences. Be sure to cite scholars from a variety of backgrounds. In most fields, a dominant group is overrepresented in doctrinal materials. Thus it is important to seek out, cite and use work from a variety of ethnicities, sexuality and gender expressions, international perspectives and political points of view. Also, consider collaborating with a diverse group of faculty members live or virtually to build a repository of authentic diverse examples that will help promote cognitive presence in your online environment.

> "Minds are like parachutes, they only function when they are open."
> James Dewar

REFERENCES

Anderson, T. (2017). "How communities of inquiry drive teaching and learning in the digital age". Contact North. Available at: https://teachonline.ca/sites/default/files/pdf/enewsletters/how_communities_of_inquiry_drive_teaching_and_learning_in_the_digital.pdf.

Baker, R., Dee, T. S., Evans, B., & John, J. (2018, April 27). "Race and gender biases appear in online education". *Brookings*. Retrieved September 13, 2021, from https://www.brookings.edu/blog/brown-center-chalkboard/2018/04/27/race-and-gender-biases-appear-in-online-education/.

Becker, M. et al. (2014). "Cultural bases for self-evaluation: Seeing oneself positively in different cultural contexts". Personality and Social Psychology Bulletin, DOI: 10.1177/0146167214522836.

Bektashi, L. (2018). "Community of Inquiry Bokashi in online learning: Use of technology". In *Technology and the Curriculum: Summer 2018*. Pressbooks. Available at: https://techandcurriculum.pressbooks.com/chapter/coi-and-online-learning/.

Black, P., & Wiliam, D. (2009). "Developing the theory of formative assessment". *Education Assessment, Evaluation and Accountability*, 21(1), pp. 5–31. Available at: https://doi.org.10.1007/s11092-008-9068-5.

CNRS (Délégation Paris Michel-Ange). (2014, February 24). "Culture influences young people's self-esteem: Fulfillment of value priorities of other individuals important to youth." *ScienceDaily*. Retrieved September 11, 2021, from www.sciencedaily.com/releases/2014/02/140224081027.htm.

Gebauer, J. E., Sedikides, C., Wagner, J., Bleidorn, W., Rentfrow, P. J., Potter, J., & Gosling, S. D. (2015). "Cultural norm fulfillment, interpersonal belonging, or getting ahead? A large-scale cross-cultural test of three perspectives on the function of self-esteem". *Journal of Personality and Social Psychology*, 109(3), pp. 526–48. Available at: https://doi.org/10.1037/pspp0000052.supp (Supplemental).

Golia, M. (n.d.). "Course design as teaching presence in online courses" [blog]. *Rochester Institute of Technology*. Available at: https://www.rit.edu/academicaffairs/tls/course-design-teaching-presence-online-courses.

Granite State College. (n.d.). "Early online engagement strategies". Available at: https://faculty.granite.edu/wp-content/uploads/COVID19 _TeachingStrategies/Early-Engagement-Strategies-1.pdf.

Hall, S. (1982). "The classroom climate: A chilly one for women?" Washington D.C.: Association of American Colleges.

Hanover Research (2014, August). *The Impact of Formative Assessment and Learning Intentions on Student Achievement.* Available at: https://www .hanoverresearch.com/media/The-Impact-of-Formative-Assessment-and-Learning -Intentions-on-Student-Achievement.pdf.

Hanson, M. (2021, July 10). "Online education statistics [Report]". *EducationData. org.* Available at: https://educationdata.org/online-education-statistics.

Hawkins, B., Morris, M., Nguyen, T., Siegel, J., & Vardell, E. (2017). "Advancing the conversation: Next steps for lesbian, gay, bisexual, trans, and queer (LGBTQ) health sciences librarianship". *Journal of the Medical Library Association*, 105. 10.5195/JMLA.2017.206. [Johns Hopkins Diversity Wheel Source Publication]. Available at: https://www.researchgate.net/figure/ Diversity-Wheel-as-used-at-Johns-Hopkins-University-12_fig1_320178286.

Humphrey, D. L., & Davis, C. (2021, May 11). "The future started yesterday and we're already late. A case for antiracist online teaching". *Journal of Interactive Technology and Pedagogy,* 19(1). Available at: https://jitp.commons.gc.cuny .edu/the-future-started-yesterday-and-were-already-late-the-case-for-antiracist- online-teaching/.

Jaschik, S. (2018, March 8). "Race and gender bias in online courses". *Inside Higher Education.* Available at: https://www.insidehighered.com/news/2018/ 03/08/study-finds-evidence-racial-and-gender-bias-online-education.

Jones-Roberts, C. A. (2018). "Increasing social presence online: Five strategies for instructors". *FDLA Journal* 3, Article 8. Available at: https://nsuworks .nova.edu/cgi/viewcontent.cgi?article=1018&context=fdla-journal.

Matias. (2021, November 17). *NCES blog.* IES. Retrieved March 2, 2022, from https://nces.ed.gov/blogs/nces/post/research-roundup-nces-celebrates-native- american-heritage-month.

Sezgin, S. (2021, January). "Cognitive relations in online learning: Challenge of cognitive presence and participation in online discussions based on cognitive style". *Participatory Educational Research*, 8(1), pp. 344–61. Available at: http://dx.doi.org/10.17275/per.21.20.8.1.

UDL (n.d.). UDL On Campus: "About UDL". Retrieved September 13, 2021, from http://udloncampus.cast.org/page/udl_about.

Ward Oda, C., Stanley, L., & Graham, G. (n.d.). "Research and relevance to the field" [Interviews]. *Capella University.* Available at: https://media.capella .edu/CourseMedia/ed5006element233861/wrapper.asp.

5.   Accessibility tools

Monica Sanders

I   INTRODUCTION

Earlier we discussed access to the Internet and courses as a factor in creating engaging and inclusive online courses. You learned about some of the tools you can use in this kind of classroom and ways to make access less of a factor in educational opportunity. Now, we will discuss accessibility as a factor of equity, inclusion and engagement in the online classroom. There are ways to engage every kind of learning style while cultivating learning and digital citizenship. In 2021, *Inside Higher Ed* conducted a survey of instructors from more than 20 higher education institutions about their preparation for creating an Americans with Disabilities Act compliant course during the transition to digital learning. 75% of the respondents reported that they had not received any training or resources (see https://www.insidehighered.com/advice/2020/09/02/making-accessibility-priority-online-teaching-even-during-pandemic-opinion).

II   ACCESS AS AN EQUITY ISSUE

As noted by the aforementioned study, this is both a systemic higher education issue as well as a course design challenge. Technology, wider use of the Internet and digital tools generally have made access to higher education more democratized. Unfortunately, the conversation around opening the space has been about opening the space to more students generally. There is a need for further improvements to the underlying philosophy around ensuring digital accessibility for students. That need should be about not just opening the space, but making sure it is one that everyone can access and is accessible to everyone.

In some cases, universities are passing rules and requiring specific outcomes to address equity, accessibility and availability of tools in course design. Yale for example requires that all digital content, in courses or otherwise, should be accessible to people with visual, cognitive, learning, neurological, physical, or speech disabilities. Appropriately for the nature of the school, the Texas Tech University Health Sciences Center in El Paso conducted an accessibility review of its digital properties. It then overhauled its websites, videos, LMSs and apps to ensure all students could access them. In Australia, the Royal Melbourne Institute of Technology has implemented a Digital Accessibility Framework, which sets "design standards for accessibility of all digital resources [and] outlining roles and responsibilities for compliance" (Linney, 2020). Passing clear standards is an institutional approach which forebears good outcomes for students.

Whether your institution has such rules with which to comply, voluntary guidelines or has a departmental or individual approach, design is still key. Consistent with the scholarship of teaching and learning, the approach to course design and accessibility is to consider the outcome, the learners' needs, and then how learners can get to the outcome without unnecessary barriers. When we choose options, center students or provide flexibility for learners, we enhance accessibility. As opposed to the flipped classroom many of us know, equitable design requires a flipped philosophical approach. Thus, instead of designing for people without barriers, design for those with barriers and create an environment that addresses multiple needs at once (Parsi, 2021).

If equity and inclusion are important parts of online learning, then part of accomplishing this goal is understanding that good, universal design is just as important as tools and good Internet access. The first two principles of universal design are equity and flexibility. Both of these are reflected in the approach that is guided by the more universal and broader Internet oriented Web Content Accessibility Guidelines (WCAG, 2021). The guidelines were created by a group of international experts through a consensus process and are therefore considered to be universally applicable. They are meant to standardize the concept of accessibility. It is organized by levels. The WCAG level two is the minimum standard to comply with Section 508 of the Americans with Disabilities Act. This means that certain access tools are required by law. The requirements coincide with noted digital barriers which include: videos without captioning or audio that is not transcribed, text and pages that cannot be resized or poor contrast between colors on web pages or between photos. However, many of these guidelines are focused on a subset of disabilities such as mobility, vision and hearing impairments. There are a broader range of challenges to be addressed, starting with design.

III   WHY IS IT IMPORTANT TO INCORPORATE GOOD DESIGN AS MUCH AS IT IS TO HAVE ACCESS AND ACCESSIBILITY?

Numerous outlets and researchers have said that the educational environment is one where civil rights is still an issue. They cite the *Brown v. Board* case and note that representation is a goal we are still missing in this country. There is racial stratification in our schools, as well as gender issues still to be resolved. Fortunately, the spectrum of cognitive challenges and disabilities is more presently part of this larger conversation. And it should be, given that we have and will continue to discuss the legal requirements for accessibility in addition to provisions concerning non-discrimination in education. As discussed in the inclusion and engagement chapters, representation via multiple means, expression focused on students, as well as health engagement, are all parts of universal design. This helps students as well as instructors.

Universal design is not a new concept, but its actual application varies based on institutional support. As mentioned earlier, faculty and staff often do not receive the training and institutional support they need to create courses using accessible techniques or universal design. The proof is in the outcomes. Recent studies pointed out some of the most common issues are that learning management systems (LMS) and certain kinds of content on those platforms are not optimized for access technologies. They are not designed in a way that contemplates Internet access issues. And when it comes to content, there are examples of nonconforming choices such as Flash-based tools or photocopied images of text in a PDF (Smith et al., 2020). One is not compatible with screen readers, and addition to this challenge, the other does not always load properly in mobile only environments.

Understanding and unpacking the challenges is an important part of addressing them. The goal is to create an overall culture of inclusion. Researchers at Northwestern University have said that disabled students find online courses more appealing. One of the reasons is online courses' ability to provide greater flexibility. They are easier to access for students with mobility issues, who can work from their homes instead of trying to navigate inaccessible campuses, classrooms and bathrooms at older institutions. Particularly with asynchronous classes, students can work at their own pace, allowing students to do their work when they are most comfortable and prepared, rather than when the class is scheduled (Smith et al., 2020).

According to Roberts and Crittenden, approximately 70% of online students with disabilities do not disclose their disability or request accommodations (Roberts et al., 2011). Sometimes the issue is institutional communication; students may not be aware of the support that is available to them. For others it is a choice involving a desire for inclusion and non-judgment. They choose not to disclose because they want "the opportunity to allow intellect, skill, and character to become their observed identity, rather than their disability".[2] This heightens the need for online courses to be designed for accessibility from the beginning. That way all students can engage with the course materials and the instructor without having to choose between maintaining their privacy and passing a class. Building an accessible course allows them to have both (Roberts et al., 2011).

One of the first steps to achieving this goal is to take a hard look at the LMS itself (Lieberman, 2018). Two of the more widely used options, Blackboard and Canvas, have accessibility features that allow faculty, instructors and institutions to analyze the accessibility features of the systems. They can also provide an analysis of content being used in a specific course. Those are Blackboard's Ally (Ally) and Canvas' Accessibility Checker. The University of Central Florida also offers an open-source tool called Udoit which can be used to review courses or programs for progress. Any of these tools works mainly by being embedded into the institution's LMS.

Ally works by running materials through a checklist of common accessibility issues. Based on the presence of challenges or lack of them, it assigns an "accessibility score" between one and 100 to each. First, this is a rating or grading system that is familiar to educators and easy to interpret. Second, it directs the user towards a goal of identifying and understanding areas where improvements are needed and then suggests a road map to greater accessibility. For some versions, it can generate ideas for additional resources (such as mobile versions of documents) that can make a course more accessible. Udoit is an open-source tool available from the University of Central Florida's Center for Distributed Learning and Student Accessibility Services. However, it is funded in part by Instructure, the developer for Canvas. The tool analyzes the distinct parts of courses: announcements, assignments, discussions, files, pages, syllabi, embeds and module URLs. It also rates them for accessibility, but does not offer a score. What it does is use parameters and review the items. There are some materials that are outside its purview, those include external documents and some video/audio files.

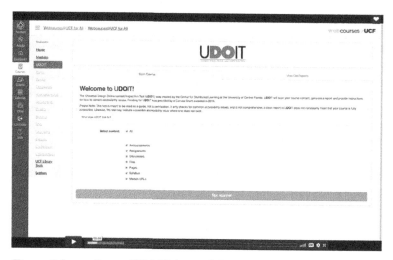

Figure 5.1   Image UDOIT Accessibility Toolkit

Despite their limitations, any of these tools are good for helping faculty and their institutions identify issues and curate appropriate solutions.

Now that we understand how to address accessibility challenges as well as have some tools by which we can identify them, let's look at how to deal with specific accessibility issues. First, approach the course with the mindset that we as instructors must account for a variety of learning styles in the educational environment. For example, some students are visual learners or spatial learners. This means they perform better when color, layout and images are used as core parts of lectures and boards. Teaching with images, videos, slides and other visual presentations is a good tactic to help this kind of learner online. Other students, for a variety of reasons, are more auditory learners and prefer audio lessons like recorded lectures, the aforementioned flipped classroom and podcasts. For many of them, the gold standard is being verbally addressed in face-to-face lessons (Lynch, 2020).

In addition to personal engagement, thoughtful design and using external tools to address/enhance accessibility, offer content in multiple formats, such as video and text or text and boxes or graphics. Generally, in addition to the screen readers and magnifiers mentioned earlier, part of any institution's basic toolkit of accessibility tools should include transcription and closed captioning, both of which come with most Zoom subscriptions. They can be added for a low cost to messaging applications like Slack or Microsoft Teams. Refreshable braille applications and assisted reading applications are also important for students with visual impairments and are free or low cost to add to learning management systems (Taylor, 2021).

IV   VISUAL IMPAIRMENT

One way to help students with visual impairments is to convert PowerPoint to HTML to support browser applications and add-ins like Word Talk (Rodríguez et al., 2006). This is a free add-in for Microsoft Word that can read any Word document aloud. It can also create audio files that can be saved. Assistive technology expert Paul Hamilton writes that "WordTalk functions can be accessed by customizable keyboard shortcuts for individuals with vision challenges, or those who cannot use a mouse effectively, or to speed the work of anyone who relies extensively on WordTalk." In addition, students with reading disabilities can also use screen readers to help them understand course materials. In an in-person classroom, when working with visually impaired students, it is important to have clear pathways to destinations and a clutter-free environment. Online the approach is similar, try to keep LMS pages straightforward with clear headings and few attachments. Label modules clearly and succinctly. Try to avoid multi-level and complicated groupings of topics and assignments. This helps students using Braille keyboards and screen readers. For students with other disabilities, it helps them by offering an easy to navigate environment.

V   HEARING IMPAIRMENT

For students with hearing issues, there is one simple rule: if the content is auditory, make it visual, and if it is visual, make it auditory. For auditory disabilities, there is one easy fix, use Zoom's automatic captioning service or try to add closed captions to recorded lectures and videos. Be sure to have captions and descriptors for graphics and photos. Some LMS will allow you to add this onto your class in the portal. Make sure you use a microphone, AirPods or another voice amplification device to ensure your voice is coming across as clearly as possible. This will help with students' ability to hear generally as well as those with impairments. The captioning services are more accurate with clearer voices. Be sure to supplement auditory materials with visuals and written documents. That can be posting syllabi or even making your lecture notes available after each class.

VI   MOBILITY LIMITATIONS

For students with limited mobility, FaceMouse turns a standard webcam into a mouse operator. This allows students to use their head and facial gestures to perform a number of tasks, including pointing the cursor, clicking on sites, or typing on the keyboard.

The user's head and face functions like a remote "joystick" or controller. The sensitivity level can vary to make it easier to control. Specific head or facial actions can be linked to keyboard presses. "Head Down" can be assigned as the "Down Cursor", and "Mouth Open" could be "Enter Key". All the various face actions can be assigned to a keystroke (Staff & About the Author TeachThought Staff, 2015).

Another approach to dealing with mobility issues is that the manipulation and navigation of content can be controlled through available alternative voluntary actions (e.g., head movements, vocal command, puff or sip, for students with paralysis or reduced dexterity).

Rapid prototyping tools allow the rapid customization of physical materials and tools. These include holders, handles, stabilizers, switches, buttons, and device casings to make controls easier to hold and manipulate (Buehler et al., 2014). Internet of things sensors, monitors and actuators enable the creation of smart environments that can be responsive to diverse personal needs (e.g., controlling light, heat and security) (Domingo, 2012).

So far, we have discussed students with "visible" disabilities, but another challenge is the recognition and offering of resources and assistance to students with "invisible" disabilities. An invisible disability is one that is not visually apparent, "but impacts an individual's ability to go to work, study, socialize, and otherwise participate in society" (Griffin, 2019). Although the disability itself creates a challenge for the person who has it, they must often deal with how others fail to recognize, acknowledge, or accommodate their disability. There is a cascading impact of exclusion for these students.

Some examples of invisible disabilities include:

- Mental health conditions like anxiety, depression, bipolar disorder, post-traumatic stress disorder, etc.
- Learning disabilities such as Dyslexia, ADD, ADHD, etc.
- Neurological conditions like Auditory Neuropathy Spectrum Disorder, Autism Spectrum Disorder, Traumatic Brain Injuries, etc.
- Autoimmune disorders like Fibromyalgia, Crohn's Disease, Lupus, HIV, etc.
- Chronic fatigue.
- Chronic pain from migraines, injury, arthritis, carpal tunnel syndrome, etc.

Part of our understanding of invisible disabilities is understanding they are not rare. For example, dyslexia affects about 10% of the world in some way. Students with dyslexia benefit from the use of graphics, charts and other visualizations that enhance the meaning of text. If you make sure that text is captioned, then making this change to your course design helps students with hearing impairments and dyslexia, without excluding the visually impaired. Use larger fonts, between 12 and 14 points to increase readability. Avoid justifying text or using any formatting that creates uneven spaces between words and paragraphs as that can aggravate the impact dyslexia has on reading comprehension. This is a part of the population that has a growing advocacy community that, among other things, shares tools to help with dyslexia accommodations. You can get more information from the American or British dyslexia associations.

Many students are also affected by Attention Deficit Hyperactivity Disorder (ADHD). This is a chronic disorder that leads to a lack of attention, hyperactivity, and impulsiveness (Lynch, 2020). Another part of our work to understand such invisible disabilities is knowing how lack of accommodation impacts affected students. They can appear to have poor social skills, some may show more severe problems such as drug or alcohol abuse (Wolf, 2006). Often the result for these students is punitive rather than assistive. Being assistive to students with ADHD is to be engaging and clear. For students with issues following along or paying attention, using diverse assignments and a variety of approaches to the delivery of materials is a helpful accommodation. We will discuss that further in Chapter 7. Some other techniques include providing syllabuses with clear assignment descriptions and deadlines and open and close lectures with reviews and summaries. This is an assistive approach for some students, but layered learning for everyone in the class. Understanding how to incorporate new techniques is just a start to working with neuro-diverse students.

One example of the issue of under recognition of neurodivergent or neurodiverse students is illustrated by their experience during the COVID-19 pandemic. Many reported that the transition to home-based learning did not account for the structure the classroom provided to students with ADHD and other disabilities. Understanding and being attentive to complex ideas on a video screen was also a prevalent issue. The first problem was not understanding that the concept of neurodivergence and neurodiversity is a paradigm that acknowledges and accepts different ways of thinking and acting. "It's a diversity and inclusion perspective applied to autism, ADHD, learning disabilities and other invisible disabilities" said Solvegi Shmulsky, a professor and director of the Center for Neurodiversity at Landmark College, a Vermont institution that specializes in serving students with learning disabilities (St. Amour, 2020). There are some easy to implement and accessible design techniques and means of presenting course materials that can be helpful to a variety of neurodiverse students, which include:

- Structure content with headings and bulleted lists.
- Use labels consistently.
- Make your page layout simple, avoid distracting images and animations.
- Ensure that due dates for assignments are clearly stated and easily located in the course.
- Break large assignments down into components.
- Give feedback on each submitted component in a reasonable amount of time before the next one is due. (Griffin, 2019)

Three of the so-called "Big Tech" companies have websites about accessibility or inclusive design. Google's Accessibility website (https://support.google.com/a/answer/2821355?hl=en&ref_topic=3035040) has tutorials about how to incorporate screen readers, keyboard access and color controls into all of its products. There is a template for classroom use that includes tips about "focus order" which is a way of designing courses that can be particularly helpful to students with attention disorders. Microsoft's site (https://www.microsoft.com/design/inclusive/) has an introduction to universal design and inclusion principles for educators and leaders of any kind who are interested in the topic. There is also a toolkit available that includes activity cards. One exercise is to create a "persona spectrum" to understand the wide range of challenges, understand how those challenges impact a person's experiences and the way design can minimize those impacts. Apple's accessibility site (https://www.apple.com/accessibility/) also has accessibility templates available to the public. The company mainly highlights the standard Apple features, such as dictation options, that help with attention issues, but are actually accessible design. The company claims that accessibility features should be "normal" features.

To make accessibility normative, model good accessibility habits during discussion groups and live classes. Many online instructors use discussions as an important teaching and learning tool (Stavredes, 2011). Discussions and discussion boards in asynchronous classes are great ways to add variety to assignments and support socialization among students. For some, these kinds of interaction can be intimidating, especially for neurodiverse students. As such, it is important for instructors to teach and model discussion board etiquette.

Organizing discussions topics in advance so that students can keep track of topics is important. This will help a wide variety of students with disabilities, but also help the class better prepare for how they will interact with their colleagues in these spaces. Make sure the parameters of the discussion are clear. Post any supplemental materials as links and attachments. Write clear instructions about the goal of the discussion. If the students are to come up with a solution to a problem, make both the problem and the range of potential solutions clear. If it is to be open-ended, help students understand as much. And finally, write an online etiquette statement that includes language that reinforces any other inclusion and accommodation statements you may have posted in other parts of the course.

VII GETTING SUPPORT, WORKING WITH DISABILITIES SERVICES AND CHIEF DIVERSITY OFFICERS

Finally, do not leave out other important parts of the overall inclusion and access team at your institution. Those include student affairs of the office of disability services, which can help you with choosing tools and approaches to accommodate a wide variety of students. The chief diversity officer or office of diversity, equity and inclusion will also have resources such as articles and tools about diversity and inclusion, some of which will complement those discussed earlier in this book. Both of these kinds of professionals are highly skilled at making sure the Americans with Disabilities Act (ADA) and the 2008 changes to it, the Americans with Disabilities Act Amendment Act (ADAAA) are part of university procedures. That includes course development. The ADAAA expanded what it means to be disabled. One of the purposes for the changes was to include invisible disabilities and to include measures to make web pages and online systems more accessible. Because of these changes, more people, more students are protected under the ADA and other federal and state laws against discrimination. Educational institutions are federally required to make accommodations for these individuals.

Ultimately, the solution to access and accessibility issues is to take a framework level approach that prioritizes universal approaches with targeted support. Students generally will respond well to classes that are inclusive, which means better participation, enrollment and engagement. Institutions have a responsibility to prepare all students to meet their full potential and become prosperous, self-guided contributors to our global community. Perhaps considering students with learning differences may be the impetus that pushes some parts of the higher education system closer to a principles framework approach. But there are other needs to consider as well.

Just as access, representation and inclusion are important parts of creating an engaging learning environment, understanding students' well-being is important. Part of this is understanding their workload. Alongside access and accessibility, is understanding how different approaches to learning and different learning environments necessitate different approaches to course management and workload.

REFERENCES

Buehler, E., Hurst, A., & Hofmann, M. (2014). "Coming to grips: 3D printing for accessibility", in *Proceedings of the 16th international ACM SIGACCESS conference on Computers & accessibility (ASSETS '14)*. Association for Computing Machinery, New York, NY, USA, pp. 291–2. DOI: https://doi.org/10.1145/2661334.2661345.

Griffin, E. (2019, June 3). "Tips for accommodating invisible disabilities in elearning". *3Play Media*. Available at: https://www.3playmedia.com/blog/tips-for-accommodating-invisible-disabilities-in-elearning/.

Lieberman, M. (2018, May 1). "Technology can help address accessibility challenges, but many say it's an incomplete solution". *Inside Higher Ed.* Available at: https://www.insidehighered.com/digital-learning/article/2018/05/02/technology-can-help-address-accessibility-challenges-many-say.

Linney, S. (2020, March 30). "Why digital accessibility is essential in higher education". *QS*. Available at: https://www.qs.com/why-digital-accessibility-is-essential-in-higher-education/.

Lynch, M. (2020, November 18). "Why designing for accessibility in e-learning matters". *The Tech Edvocate*. Available at: https://www.thetechedvocate.org/why-designing-for-accessibility-in-e-learning-matters/.

Northwestern University. (n.d.). Distance Learning: School of Professional Studies: Northwestern University, "Why is web accessibility important?". *Northwestern University School of Professional Studies: School of Professional Studies*. Available at: https://sps.northwestern.edu/distance-learning/how-do-i/course-accessible/why-is-web-accessibility-important.php.

Parsi, N. (2021, June 15). "Rethinking technology accessibility in higher ed: Technology solutions that drive education". Available at: https://edtechmagazine.com/higher/article/2021/03/rethinking-technology-accessibility-higher-ed-perfcon.

Roberts, J., Crittenden, L., & Crittenden, J. (2011). "Students with disabilities and online learning: A cross-institutional study of perceived satisfaction with accessibility compliance and service". *Internet and Higher Education*, 14, pp. 242–50.

Rodríguez, E. P. G., Domingo, M. G., Ribera, J. P., Hill, M. A., & Jardí, L. S. (2006). "Usability for all: Towards improving the e-learning experience for visually impaired users", in Miesenberger, K., Klaus, J., Zagler, W. L., & Karshmer, A. I. (eds), *Computers Helping People with Special Needs*. ICCHP 2006. Lecture Notes in Computer Science, vol 4061. Springer, Berlin, Heidelberg. Available at: https://doi.org/10.1007/11788713_189.

Smith, M., Pennault, L., Tosch, K., & Marcus, D. (2020, September 30). "Making accessibility a priority in online teaching even during a pandemic" (opinion). Available at: https://www.insidehighered.com/print/advice/2020/09/02/making-accessibility-priority-online-teaching-even-during-pandemic-opinion.

St. Amour, M. (2020, May 13). "Neurodivergent students face challenges in the quick switch to remote learning". Available at: https://www.insidehighered.com/news/2020/05/13/neurodivergent-students-face-challenges-quick-switch-remote-learning.

Staff, T. T., & About the Author TeachThought Staff (TeachThought is an organization dedicated to innovation in education through the growth of outstanding teachers). (2015, December 9). "8 helpful assistive technology tools for your classroom". *TeachThought*. Available at: https://www.teachthought.com/technology/8-helpful-assistive-technology-tools-for-your-classroom/.

Stavredes, T. (2011, June 30). "Effective online teaching: Foundations and strategies for student success". Retrieved March 2, 2022, from https://eric.ed.gov/?id=ED522106.

Taylor, R. (2021, March 9). "7 web accessibility resources every college with distance learning needs". *Rev*. Available at: https://www.rev.com/blog/7-web-accessibility-resources-every-college-with-distance-learning-needs.

WCAG (2021, August 18). "Web content accessibility guidelines – What is WCAG?" *eSSENTIAL Accessibility*. Available at: https://www.essentialaccessibility.com/blog/web-content-accessibility-guidelines-wcag.

Wolf, L. E. (2006, January 25). "College students with ADHD and other hidden disabilities". *Nyas publications*. The New York Academy of Sciences. Available at: https://nyaspubs.onlinelibrary.wiley.com/doi/10.1111/j.1749 -6632.2001.tb05792.x.

6. Managing pace and workload in online courses

Susannah McGowan

I   INTRODUCTION

During the 2020–2021 pandemic in the United States, higher education in many states pivoted online to minimize the spread of COVID-19. Since March 2020, centers for teaching and learning responded to new challenges to support faculty in planning their online courses. Each semester's challenges shifted and evolved as faculty and students adapted to the virtual environment. Persistent questions about balancing asynchronous time and synchronous time existed each semester resulting in multiple discussions about pacing the workload, reimagining assessment options, and developing productive structure for class time. Coming out of a year with the vast majority of Georgetown faculty teaching online, this chapter presents findings around the strategies and approaches that supported student learning. This chapter provides a snapshot of one center's response to pandemic pedagogy, the existing principles that supported the response, and practical suggestions for teaching and learning to endure in post-pandemic higher education.

II   GEORGETOWN'S CONTEXT

Georgetown University switched to remote learning in March 2020 as the COVID-19 pandemic hit the United States. The center for teaching and learning at Georgetown, Center for New Designs in Learning and Scholarship (CNDLS), which serves as both a center for teaching and learning as well as a center for digital learning and online programs, responded quickly with tailored workshops and webinars that evolved each semester depending on the needs of the community. Examples of support included a virtual conference on digital pedagogy in May 2020,

Table 6.1   Faculty participation in CNDLS programs

Summer 2020	Teaching, Learning, & Innovation Summer Institute	Course Design Institute	Digital Learning Days	Individual Consultations	Unique Faculty Overall
Faculty Participation in CNDLS Programs	907	1137	279	516	1856

a series of department-based Course Design Institutes (CDI) throughout the summer where faculty engaged with online course design principles and effective, inclusive pedagogical practices; and a series of tailored workshops on select teaching topics such as alternative assessments and group work in Zoom, our virtual conferencing software. We worked with over 1,850 faculty and staff members in Summer 2020.

CNDLS designed and delivered programming throughout summer 2020 to prepare faculty for flexible and adaptive remote teaching. CNDLS staff includes faculty developers, instructional designers, technology specialists, media producers, diversity and inclusion experts, web developers, and graduate assistants who worked closely over the summer to deliver effective and efficient programming.

CNDLS' focus during the pandemic semesters followed four main objectives for supporting faculty and graduate students while giving faculty a deeper dive into remote learning in order to prepare for the fall semester's both online and hybrid modalities. Our objectives were:

- Planning: adapt their syllabus and semester plan for remote learning.
- Engagement: adopt intentional teaching practices that focus on engagement, responsiveness, community, inclusivity, and flexibility in an online environment.
- Effective technology: meaningfully integrate technology to give students a rich learning experience.
- Connection to mission: consider what a "signature" Georgetown course looks like online.

The objectives outlined the commitment to supporting faculty not only in the use of tools like Canvas and Zoom, but also in basic course design practices with a strong emphasis on active learning (Theobald et al.,

2020; Tanner, 2013). Although the CDI design was intentional and effective, we determined after the first two weeks that we could leverage our synchronous time with faculty to discuss more important themes. As faculty grappled with new technologies, they were less likely to consider pedagogical choices for student learning in the virtual environment. Many faculty expressed concerns about the complexity of adapting their teaching for a remote mode where they had to make choices never thought of before: to deliver information synchronously and asynchronously to students across multiple time zones; facilitate discussion in Zoom, manage Zoom functionality such as the chat feature, sharing slides, and how to maintain engagement. From this extended level of engagement with faculty, CNDLS engaged in many conversations about teaching and what was most effective for students in the virtual environment.

As the academic year progressed, CNDLS took part in rapid evaluation efforts to gauge faculty and student responses to the virtual learning environment. On the faculty side of teaching and learning, their concerns changed from semester to semester culminating in practices and strategies aimed to balance pace and workload for faculty and students alike. A quick synopsis of what was learned during the academic year 2020–2021 contributed to practices and concerns to take into account when working in any online environment – in or beyond a global pandemic.

Spring 2020 represented a total focus on understanding Canvas and how to organize materials within Canvas effectively. The transition to virtual, synchronous sessions entailed orienting faculty and students to common functionalities within Zoom. From frequent student surveys, there emerged a persistent concern over engagement and the inability to engage students effectively in the virtual environment.

As we moved from spring to June, summer virtual efforts focused on how to best prepare for a Fall semester where the modality of the semester was not announced until the end of July 2020. Intensive, weekly summer course design institutes explored course design, technological tools for engagement, and active learning activities to incorporate into a syllabus for the Fall. In each departmental engagement, CNDLS facilitators outlined and discussed each modality with faculty members. On the affective side of the experience, faculty, staff, and students participating in fall planning were showing signs of pandemic burnout and planning fatigue for the fall. Early signs emerged around managing workload and pacing as potential concerns amidst the uncertainty and Zoom fatigue.

Fall 2020 faculty focus groups represented efforts to connect to students through pre-surveys, consistent feedback, and transparent assignments and activities. In conversations with over 60 faculty members, we learned the following practices were effective in the virtual environment:

- Holding virtual office hours via multiple platforms and at flexible times.
- Soliciting frequent student feedback about student needs, their learning environments, and creating connections with students.
- Using synchronous time for group work using Zoom breakout rooms and collaborative document tools such as Google Docs and Google Jamboard.
- Improving course organization and use of asynchronous discussion boards via Canvas.
- Recording and facilitating virtual class using Zoom when students, instructors, or guest speakers are remote.

Persistent concerns among faculty included:

- Everything about teaching takes longer in the virtual environment, contributing to a sense of greater faculty workload and less balance with research activities.
- Gauging and creating student engagement in Zoom is a struggle.
- Teaching during a pandemic is emotionally taxing for faculty.
- Time zone management has no great synchronous solution.

Preparation for Spring 2021 semester emphasized planning and syllabus design in alignment with university directives on making space for students and lightening the load on course work, essentially advocating for a more focused attention on pacing and workload issues. At the end of the spring semester, three themes emerged among practices faculty reported as being instrumental to their pacing and their focus on students: flexibility, fostering community, and an emphasis on intentional, purposeful structuring of time.

A   What Informs This Work

The theoretical basis for preparing faculty for online teaching and learning stemmed from years of online learning research and developing online programs within CNDLS. Backward design, universal learning design, and emergent hyflex learning literature informed the practices faculty were encouraged to implement during pandemic teaching support.

III   BACKWARD DESIGN: COURSE DESIGN FOR STUDENT LEARNING

Backwards design (Wiggins & McTighe, 2005) is a simple template for course design that requires in-depth reflection around course choices for student learning to bring into instructional practice. This is student-centered design prompting instructors to consider what students need to know and do by the end of the course. The authors are clear that this is not a pedagogical approach or prescriptive program (like other instructional design models). The basic premise is to identify goals, identify student evidence that students meet these goals, and the design of instructional activities that contain the assessment and the goal. To differentiate the type of goals one may have for students, the backward design model employs a three-tiered model to discuss the enduring understanding, what is important to know, and what is worthwhile to know. Staying true to the backward design framework is thinking about what is feasible within a given amount of time, what is essential to take away from the course, then from there sift through what else is important and what would be worthwhile for the students to know.

IV   PROFESSIONAL DEVELOPMENT FOR DIGITAL LEARNING

Ingenuity, effort, transformation, and rethinking of one's teaching approach for an online environment are lofty goals for any professional development program, not to mention one designed during a pandemic. The amount of intellectual investment in online teaching shows that this "… is not something that can easily be picked up along the way as some-thing to be done off the side of the desk while engaged in important or time-consuming activities such as research" (Weaver & Robbie, 2008). It is necessary to structure opportunities for faculty to consider using tech-nology effectively to support their goals for student learning. Established frameworks for preparing faculty and graduate students to teach online include setting up processes and conversations to help instructors trans-form their classroom approaches to the affordances and limitations of online tools such as the learning management system, balancing asyn-chronous and synchronous time, and finding other forms of engagement

(Garrison et al., 2001). Another crucial element for professional development of faculty includes fostering conversations about teaching. This is central to all of CNDLS' programs as well as the center's ethos for supporting faculty and graduate students in departmental-based cohorts for learning how to teach online during a pandemic (Debelius & Mooney, 2021). Facilitated conversations about teaching and learning, what works, what could be improved, and informal sharing of disciplinary practices proved most rewarding for faculty during the pandemic year and most productive for maintaining a focus on student learning.

V   UNIVERSAL DESIGN FOR LEARNING

Similar to backward design in the focus on student learning, Universal Design for Learning (UDL) focuses on access to materials in order for all students to, "In brief, universal design is a philosophy that argues that if you design content (e.g., a syllabus, an assignment, a lecture) for students with disabilities, you improve the content not only for those students but for all students" (Phillips & Colton, 2021). This includes decisions on how to present content and in which platform (Canvas Page, PDF, or Word Document, Google Document, etc.); as well as enabling closed captions on videos. The main principles encourage instructors to provide to students multiple means of representation in course content, multiple means of engagement, and multiple ways to express and apply knowledge learned (CNDLS, n.d.).

VI   FOUR DESIGN FACTORS FOR PACING ONLINE COURSES

Within Georgetown's context of the pandemic pivot, implementing effective strategies for pace and workload developed over three semesters. The following factors were important design choices faculty needed to consider for the virtual environment for pacing: synchronous versus asynchronous time, intentional structuring of synchronous time, punctuating the semester with relevant coursework, and an examination of the assignments and assessments necessary for students to complete. These four factors not only encompassed many discussions between CNDLS staff and faculty, these factors were also identified as practices to retain from the pandemic academic year to the return to in-person courses.

A   Balancing Asynchronous vs Synchronous Time

Prior to fall 2020 semester, Georgetown's decision to remain virtual for fall came in late July as CNDLS continued its series of intensive, departmental-based course design institutes. At that time, we committed to preparing faculty for all instructional eventualities: completely remote, hybrid/hyflex, or in-person. This included answering the recurring question of how to manage a balance between how class time is used and what is manageable for students to do outside of class. Dan Levy (2020) boils this dilemma down to the simple question, "What [do] you think is the comparative advantage of a live class session over activities your students can do asynchronously? In other words, for what learning activities does being together make a difference?"

Summer 2020 was a time where many universities had not determined their fall teaching modality. At Georgetown, the conversation centered on the possibility of a fully virtual environment or a "hybrid" or "hyflex" environment. While this uncertainty posed many challenges for course planning, the hyflex model foregrounded many of the conversations around using time in constructive ways. A "hyflex" classroom environment (Beatty, 2019) represents the location of some students in the physical classroom while some students participate remotely. Even though Beatty began writing about the hyflex environment in 2006, it was a relatively unexplored modality prior to the pandemic. Figure 6.1 represents one of the visuals prepared to help faculty imagine ways to structure a hyflex environment. In an effort to help faculty imagine the physical location of students (in the classroom or projected on a screen using Zoom), it also proved useful to list activities happening in those spaces as well.

An example of this model can be found in Miller et al. (2013) who outlined the hyflex model in a statistics course. As this was one of the few studies with a focus on scholarship of teaching and learning, it proved a useful touchpoint to illustrate the hyflex classroom as well as the difference between asynchronous time and synchronous time. According to Miller, the hyflex model functions with proper support such as a teaching assistant in the room to assist in setting up classroom technology and in managing backchannel communication between online and in-person students. Slides and content are projected with at least two devices (e.g., tablet and desktop computer) with the instructor wearing a lapel microphone for maximum audio quality. Students attending online watched a live view of the instructor's computer screen, most often in full-screen

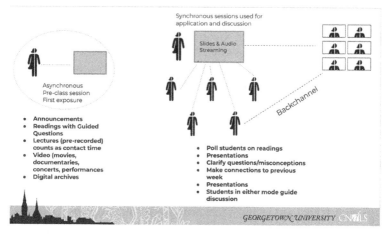

Figure 6.1   Fall 2020: Visual of a Hyflex classroom

presentation mode showing PowerPoint or Google slides with real-time writing (afforded by the tablet and stylus).

Another example of recent research on balancing time comes out of the "flipped learning" approach. "Flipped learning"1[1] or "flipped classroom" models privilege synchronous class time for community-building, collaborative and social learning while asynchronous time focuses on individual preparation, reviewing lecture content, readings, or short, formative exercises. When Georgetown faculty relied on flipped practices, this indicated intentional thinking about how students should spend their time out of class on preparatory activities and readings in order to structure the synchronous class time.

In the end, Georgetown decided to function virtually for the fall semester. However, incorporating discussions on the possibility of hyflex spurred good discussions, especially on the distinction between asynchronous and synchronous time. The illustration in Figure 6.1 demonstrated the possibilities of activities for the synchronous portion of time guiding instructors to think carefully about how to plan for a combination of lecture and student engagement while leveraging Zoom technology and functionality.

---

[1] "Flipped classroom" and "flipping" are common terms to indicate a move of additional course content to asynchronous time to create space in synchronous time for social learning activities. See Talbert, 2017a; Lo et al., 2017.

B   Strategies for Instructors to Consider Balancing Time in Online Environments

- Outline your goals for what you want students to learn and what you want them to be able to do with this knowledge.
- Determine how you want students to engage with relevant course materials.
- Incorporate readings, video lecture content, polls, and preparatory online discussion posts for asynchronous coursework.
- Dedicate class time for engagement: discussions, group activities, small group work, or guest speakers from connected fields or relevant experience.
- Devote synchronous time for students to work on independent projects with opportunities to ask questions.
- Any synchronous time can be used as any instructor uses office hours; build in opportunities for students to ask questions or receive feedback.
- Consider designating certain days or weeks as "asynchronous" in order to provide time and space for students to engage with the materials.

The accumulation of these suggestions contributes to the well-researched idea of teaching as a form of interactive facilitation rather than merely time to lecture to students (Moore, 2021).

i   Intentional structuring of course time

Faculty reflections from the 2020–2021 academic year indicated the repeated practice of aligning activities to course learning goals. In particular, faculty mentioned their increasing attention to structuring course time in ways they had not thought to do before. With the emerging theme around time, CNDLS offered a course planning studio for the Spring 2021 semester aimed to help faculty think about structuring their 15 weeks of the semester; structuring a weekly pattern or rhythm; and then structuring an engagement plan for synchronous time.

During the course planning workshop, a timeline served to visualize each week of the semester with scheduled breaks and national and religious holidays. In spring 2021, the Provost Office at Georgetown University directed faculty members to not assign anything on or near

President's Day as a way to inflect a short course reprieve ahead of the midterm point.

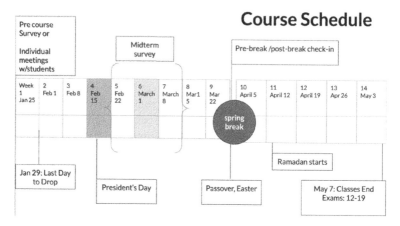

Figure 6.2   Spring 2021, sample semester by week to visualize pacing

ii   Weekly schedules

Establishing a weekly pattern to the course helps students understand what to expect within a semester in which they are taking more than three courses. Many faculty reported designating days for synchronous group activities, small group meetings, and how that time should be used. One faculty member scheduled in three asynchronous weeks to promote engaged reading and less screen time within a virtual semester.

- Establish a focus for class meeting days or for days of the week when students should focus on asynchronous activities, e.g. Mondays.
- Create limited asynchronous activities that encourage students to reduce screen time (read print books or articles, listen to audio books or podcasts, interview family members in their homes, etc.).
- Explain the support available and where to get help during the week.

iii   By class time

In our spring focus groups, researchers observed, "Some faculty reported planning out structures, prompts, and expectations for in-class group

Week 2 Schedule

	What to Do	When	Estimated Time
Preparation			
Read	Textbook: Chapter 4, pp. 26-28 PDF in Canvas, 5 pages Question Guide for Videos	Before Monday; access in Canvas Module 2	~2 hours
Watch	Videos 2-6	Before Wednesday; access in Canvas Module 2	4 x 10 min each
Activities			
Monday Sync Session	We will meet to discuss your responses to the question guide.	Monday @ 1:00pmEST (Zoom link)	50 minutes
#1 Weekly Check-in: Case Study Group	Small groups meet to reflect on themes from Monday's discussion.	Schedule this group meeting using Canvas Appointments b/w Monday and before Tuesday @8pm	50 minutes
Wednesday Sync Session	Jigsaw group discussion.	Wednesday @ 1:00pmEST (Zoom link)	50 minutes
#2 Weekly Check-in: Case Study Group	Small groups meet to reflect on themes from Wednesday's discussion and work on first case study response paper	Schedule this group meeting using Canvas Calendar Appointments between Wednesday and before Thurs @8pm	50 minutes
Friday Sync Session	Entry ticket: Identify two topics from small group meetings	Friday @ 1:00pmEST (Zoom link)	50 minutes
Assignments			
Complete Warm-Up Questions	Check your understanding of readings	Complete in Canvas Quizzes, Module 2 by Sunday @8pm	Between 15-20 minutes
Solving the Case Study: Individual Work	Apply knowledge check and video interpretation to this case study	Submit in Canvas Assignments by Thursday @5pm	45 minutes to 1 hour
Solving the Case Study: Team Work	Prepare one-page brief on your group's response to the issue	Submit in Canvas by Friday@9am	1 hour
When You Might Need Help			
Instructor Informal Drop-In Hours	Conversational time about how things are going inside and outside of course; course content; logistics	Tuesdays and Wednesdays, 10am or by appointment	However much time is needed!
Peer Mentor Sessions	Brainstorm sessions with 4th year students and fellow classmates	Monday &Wednesdays, 8pm-9pm in Zoom	

Figure 6.3　　Sample weekly schedule

work for the first time this semester upon finding unstructured breakout room time to not be as productive."

- Center your learning objectives for synchronous time on student engagement and responding to questions or material students found especially challenging.
- Plan activities to engage students from the beginning. Kevin Kelly of San Francisco State University created an open source resource with multiple examples of 50-minute, 75-minute, and 90-minute class sessions using engagement techniques such as mini-lectures, think-pair-share, polling, or minute papers (Tanner, 2013; Angelo & Cross, 2012).
- When using breakout rooms or regular group work, prepare any documents in which you want students to collaborate in, prepare specific, targeted discussion prompts, and designate how you want students to report back out to the whole class. This additional layer of structure guides students in learning how to structure group work time.

C   Strategies for Faculty to Create More Intentional Structures

- Consider what the main learning objectives will be for each week and how each synchronous class session will meet those objectives.
- Set up weekly plans to visualize the process or rhythm of the intended workflow for students.
- Indicate a suggested time range for students to complete the tasks.
- For synchronous sessions, outline the structure of your time accounting for brief lectures, group work, debriefing of group work, and spending time answering students' questions.
- For group work and team-based activities, develop specific tasks and ways to report back on how students completed those tasks; use group-generated products such as presentations or informal collection of ideas gathered in Google Docs or Slides or Jamboard.
- Access course workload calculators such to determine estimated work time for students: https://cat.wfu.edu/resources/tools/estimator2/.

VII   DESIGNING ASSIGNMENTS

In a study conducted in 2017 with university administrators on the role of technology in assessment purposes, one stakeholder noted, "students [should] have real-time and self-assessment-based ways to determine their level of success and progress toward completion. I always think about the root of the term 'assessment' as 'to sit down beside' – that sense of accompanying the learner in her or his learning journey is important" (McGowan, 2021). Implicit within this statement indicates the level to which technology, specifically a learning management system, can serve in supporting the learning journey and providing a documented, visual record of progress and feedback.

Pandemic pedagogical practices included many faculty breaking down large, weighted assignments (essays, projects, exams) into shorter, more frequent assignments. One faculty member reported converting a previous assessment into a "team test" so that students could collaborate in small groups of peers to complete it (CNDLS, Spring Report, n.d.). Giving students a choice in how they choose to complete an assignment as well as student-determined deadlines were also mentioned as adjustments made for students in the virtual environment.

All these assignment design choices contribute to pacing an online course; if larger assignments become more frequent you need to take into account the estimated time for students to complete the assignment as well as the time the instructor takes to give feedback. Student learning across a range of outcomes would benefit if faculty explored more deeply the extent to which their students fully grasped the structure, purpose, and content of their classes and assignments.

A   Strategies for Rethinking Assignments in an Online Environment

- Connect your assessments and assignments to course learning goals.
- Outline explicit assignment expectations and grading criteria.
- Provide frequent feedback opportunities to help students know where they are in their learning at strategic moments during the term, the week, or during class. Feedback can be given individually (or to smaller groups), given to the class as whole, or delivered through short videos or audio files.
- Avoid longer projects intense projects, particularly projects that do not offer frequent feedback and opportunities to revise.
- Consider alternative grading schemes that emphasize and prioritize student effort, completion, and self-pacing. "Grading for growth" emerged in 2021 as a title that encompasses many alternative grading schemes such as "mastery grading", "contract grading", "specifications grading" (Talbert, 2017b), and "ungrading" (Blum

& Kohn, 2020). The pandemic year forced faculty to examine what they wanted students to do and how they were going to communicate expectations to students as necessitating more transparency in assessment design.

VIII   PACING IN CANVAS

The Canvas learning management system (LMS) provides functionality to support pacing, access to course materials, and to outline transparent workload expectations in the "Modules" area. There are many features in Canvas to support students; however, linking to materials to access asynchronously, designing assignments and criteria, and structuring and pacing the course can best occur in Modules. Think of modules as a desktop folder on a computer or laptop. The content within that folder is relevant to that folder and it can be organized in a number of conventional ways. The same is true for Modules which act like a container for all the other elements contained in Canvas: Assignments, Discussion Boards, Pages, and media. Some faculty indicated they enabled Modules to be

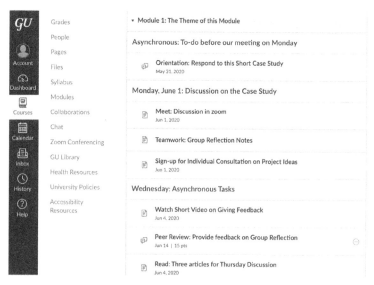

Figure 6.4   Example of a Canvas Module

their Canvas site home page (the page students see first upon entering the course site) as it served as a visual syllabus.

Using Canvas to communicate the pace of the semester became crucial for faculty to plan their semester efforts and many faculty acknowledged the added organization and structure it provided them and their students.

A   Strategies for Faculty for Online Environments

*   Use Canvas Modules for clear organization of tasks for students. Modules can be organized by weeks, units, or themes depending on your course goals.
*   Use active verbs as titles for content added to modules.
*   Use Canvas Calendar to indicate due dates for assignments allowing for automatic notifications for due dates.
*   Get to know the resources available for Canvas or any other learning management system at your institution.

IX   CONCLUSION

The pandemic academic year provided an extended snapshot of practices, implementations, and multiple efforts to maintain the academic schedule. Many of the practices outlined here were supported by research in online education prior to the pandemic, yet the skills and knowledge faculty implemented in online course design reinforced many of the findings found in research on students in digital environments. Managing pace and workload in the virtual environment requires patience, trial and error, and the ability to adapt and adjust as each semester progresses.

REFERENCES

Angelo, T. A., & Cross, K. P. (2012). *Classroom Assessment Techniques.* Jossey Bass Wiley.

Beatty, B. (2019). *Hybrid-Flexible Course Design: Implementing Student-directed Hybrid Classes.* EdTech Books. Retrieved from https://edtechbooks.org/hyflex.

Blum, S. D., & Kohn, A. (2020). *Ungrading: Why Rating Students Undermines Learning (and What to do Instead).* West Virginia University Press.

Debelius, M., & Mooney, S. (2020). "Innovation in a time of crisis: A networked approach to faculty development". *Journal on Centers for Teaching and Learning*, 12, pp. 46–67.

Garrison, D. R., Anderson, T., & Archer, W. (2001). "Critical thinking, cognitive presence, and computer conferencing in distance education". *American Journal of Distance Education*, 15(1), pp. 7–23.
Georgetown University Center for New Designs in Learning and Scholarship (CNDLS 2020). Online resources:
– Alternative Modes of Grading: https://instructionalcontinuity.georgetown.edu/pedagogies-and-strategies/alternative-grading/#labor.
– Best Practices from Pandemic Learning: https://instructionalcontinuity.georgetown.edu/guide-for-faculty/best-practices-from-pandemic-teaching-and-learning/.
– Instructional Continuity and GU: https://instructionalcontinuity.georgetown.edu/.
– Spring Faculty Discussion Sessions on Academic Engagement: https://instructionalcontinuity.georgetown.edu/wp-content/uploads/2021/07/Report_-Spring-2021-Faculty-Discussion-Sessions-on-Academic-Engagement.pdf.
– Universal Design for Learning: https://commons.georgetown.edu/teaching/design/universal-design/.
Levy, D. (2020, August 7). "The synchronous vs. asynchronous balancing act – When and how pre-work can make your live sessions stronger". Harvard Business Publishing Education: Boston, MA, USA, pp. 2–7.
Lo, C. K., Hew, K. F., & Chen, G. (2017). "Toward a set of design principles for mathematics flipped classrooms: A synthesis of research in mathematics education" *Educational Research Review*, 22(1), pp. 50–73.
McGowan, S. (2021). "Digital learning for transfer students: From definitions to applicable possibilities", in Garder, J., Koch, A., & Rosenberg, M. (eds), *The Transfer Experience: A Handbook for Creating a More Equitable and Successful Postsecondary System*. Stylus Publishing, LLC.
Miller, J., Risser, M., & Griffiths, R. (2013). "Student choice, instructor flexibility: Moving beyond the blended instructional model". *Issues and Trends in Educational Technology*, 1(1), pp. 8–24.
Moore, M. (2021). "Asynchronous discussions for first-year writers and beyond: Thinking outside the PPR (prompt, post, reply) box". Available at: https://oen.pressbooks.pub/resilientpedagogy/chapter/thinking-outside-the-ppr-prompt-post-reply-box/.
Phillips, C., & Colton, J. S. (2021). "A new normal in inclusive, usable online learning experiences". Available at: https://oen.pressbooks.pub/resilientpedagogy/chapter/chapter-9-a-new-normal-in-inclusive-usable-online-learning-experiences/.
Talbert, R. (2017a). *Flipped Learning: A Guide for Higher Education Faculty* (Stylus Publishing, LLC)
Talbert, R. (2017b). "Specifications grading: We may have a winner". Available at: https://rtalbert.org/specs-grading-iteration-winner/.
Tanner, K. D. (2013). "Structure matters: Twenty-one teaching strategies to promote student engagement and cultivate classroom equity". *CBE – Life Sciences Education*, 12(3), pp. 322–31.
Theobald, E. J., Hill, M. J., Tran, E., Agrawal, S., Arroyo, E. N., Behling, S., & Freeman, S. (2020). "Active learning narrows achievement gaps for

underrepresented students in undergraduate science, technology, engineering, and math". *Proceedings of the National Academy of Sciences*, 117(12), pp. 6476–83.

Weaver, D., & Robbie, D. (2008). "The practitioner's model: Designing a professional development program for online teaching". *International Journal on E-Learning*, 7(4), pp. 759–74.

Wiggins, G. P., & McTighe, J. (2005). *Understanding by Design*, 2nd edn. ASCD: VA, USA.

7. Apps, tools and assignment ideas for online engagement

Monica Sanders

I   OVERVIEW

Learning online does not have to mean learning in an oblivion of standardized assignments and inevitable boredom. In addition to finding new audiences for different materials, online teaching and learning offers a variety of ways to engage students. This ranges from developing digital fluency and citizenship skills in an increasingly online society, to using chalkboard proxies; working with students on gamified tools during group work to inviting a variety of presentation and assignment options.

Engagement builds community. It is important in every kind of classroom. While creating community in an online classroom may seem counterintuitive from a traditional pedagogy perspective, it is rather easy. The reason is an increasing number of students are digital natives and have social media and digital community engagement experience. The challenge is leveraging that experience to build meaningful connections and the kind of online citizenship that will help students in later stages of their education, professions and everyday life.

As our world becomes more dependent on digital infrastructure, having the skills to interact with that world is critically important. The concepts of digital fluency and digital citizenship have increasingly become part of popular conversation. Digital fluency is about being able to select, use and understand a variety of technologies (Digital Fluency in the Classroom, n.d.). This includes the social aspect of being able to interact with others while using technology. Digital citizenship is about using technology to interact with public institutions, educate or become educated and interact with communities.

While the focus on the digital aspect is new thinking, the concepts of how educators prepare students to understand language, social interactions and civic life are not new concepts. The responsibility to provide information in a way that students understand and retain is the same as any traditional approach to pedagogy would prescribe. The difference is how to achieve it in a framework with time limitations and certain limitations on social context. It starts with engagement, which we will discuss throughout this section. Part of understanding how to engage is understanding why it is necessary. To do this, we will unpack the concept of digital citizenship. Part of digital citizenship is moving from being literate to fluent, similar to learning a new language or how to write. It begins with learning how to use different tools to being able to apply the skills learned from their use to developing the capacity to use those skills in a way that respects and enhances the experiences of others (Jukes, 2015).

It is in this last piece where digital citizenship comes to bear. Part of connecting with the experiences of others is being able to navigate the nearly endless supply of information available in the digital world to learn and solve problems, be creative and collaborate. Critical thinking is necessary to analyze and make decisions about media and information involved in this particular aspect of our lives in order to be able to work authentically with others. Finally, combining all of these skills and experiences with empathy and a sense of just actions creates an engaged digital citizen (Jukes, 2015).

To quote "Digital Citizenship in Schools" by author Mark Ribble, "Students need to be educated on how to be good citizens of their country and what their rights and responsibilities are as members of society. The same issues need to be addressed with regard to the emerging digital society, so that students can learn how to be responsible and productive members of that society" (Ribble & Bailey, 2007). My approach to using tools to create an engaged classroom is about more than holding students' attention. Here we take some of the traditional concepts of skills development and civics ideas with a perspective to develop the fluency for both subject matter and public success. The online learning environment can challenge or enhance these efforts depending on the pedagogy and use of tools.

II   ONLINE DOESN'T MEAN "DISENGAGED": CREATING A VIBRANT ONLINE CLASSROOM COMMUNITY

Learning to be a good digital citizen naturally lends itself to being a good community member. Students belong to different communities. Online learning can develop all of these skills. Many students already intuitively know, but may not have developed the skills to fully actualize, that being online does not mean disengaged. Thinking about how to assist in this development has been a source of study for decades. In 2003, researchers were thinking about how to engage this author's generation, Gen "Y" online (Arhin & Johnson-Mallard, 2003). Arhin and Johnson-Mallard noted that this group of students grew up with technology and were accustomed to the rapidity with which activities can happen, describing them as "technology savvy, independent and resourceful. Conditioned to expect immediate gratification, these youth have shorter attention spans and also a low threshold for boredom". They also noted that this was a generation of people who were latchkey kids or had childcare serve as parental proxies.

This was a combination of circumstances which bred a group of people with the following traits: independence, desire for action over observation, impatience with procedure and bureaucracy developed from coming of age with the Internet. The advice for those charged with teaching this "new" tech savvy group of students: increase practical learning and classroom engagement and avoid activities and assignments involving rote memorization. Instead, challenge students to use their technological savvy in the classroom.

Juxtapose this description of "Gen Y" growing up with the Internet with "Gen Z", who have grown up with social media and will enter maturity with machine learning and artificial intelligence. There will also be differences in capacity for patience and attention spans, but also desires for outcomes and a sense of community. One group may have seen being online as a way to move faster, but this one has a sense of using it to build communities. They are also advocates, activists and other forms of digital citizens. Learning environments directed towards outcomes and confronting problems will be appealing to them. One technique for engaging with this group is the "flipped classroom".

A flipped classroom is a model where reading and other individualistic work is done at home and students work on problem solving, lab work and other experiential learning activities. Often flipped classrooms are recorded much in the way online and hybrid learning models require. A downside to this practice is that some mistake it for online videos. That is a disservice to the concept. It moves students away from rote memorization and repetition and review of readings to applying the knowledge gained from the assigned readings practically. Awidi and Paynter found that the impact of the flipped classroom benefits students in terms of motivation, increased engagement and satisfaction (Awidi & Paynter, 2019). Some of the advantages are better professor to student engagement and higher levels of interactivity. The online learning environment makes it easier to incorporate digital tools. The students can help manage some of the tools, which lessens the burden on the person teaching. Content is easy to access if incorporated into the learning management system. Approaching the class in this way is a technique to "meeting students where they are" as active, engaged digital natives. Challenge them to use their tech savvy combined with the "flipped" approach to create digital communities.

A   **Getting to Know Students Online and Helping Students to Know Each Other**

Deciding between technical and pedagogical approaches is one thing, but overcoming the missing component of knowing one another in person cannot be ignored. Because online learning takes away the casual time of just chatting before and after class, it is important to create moments for people to become familiar with each other. Icebreakers and group assignments are ideas from "in real life" that translate well online and can encourage familiarity. Here are some examples:

- One technique is to play the icebreaker game "Two Truths and a Lie" in Zoom chat. Have two or three students at a time volunteer to put three items in chat. Then use polls to have the rest of the class vote up or down on the truths versus the lies.
- Three words is another frequently used conference icebreaker. Pick a random topic, the more random the better, and give students 10–15 seconds to come up with three words to describe it. After a few minutes, ask people why they chose the words they responded with.
- An out-of-pocket question is a decidedly unconventional or weird question to lighten moods and help people get comfortable with speaking. This is one that would need to be approached with sensitiv-

ity to avoid inadvertently offending a student. The recommendation is to stay away from race, religion, gender, politics or anything similar. But also, do not hesitate to be silly. Some examples are "If you were a dog, what kind would you be and why?", "Have you ever set something on fire while cooking and what was it?", or "Name something from today that we will be nostalgic about in the future." Prior to the semester, I brainstormed some of these questions with my teaching assistants and a group of students that would not be in my class.

In addition to icebreakers, going straight to breakout rooms or small groups for team assignments also helps create community and engagement. One way to build energy in classes right out of the gate is to skip introductions and go straight to work, but make it fun. For example:

- **Take a picture of something:** You can start with something quirky such as telling each group or breakout room to take a picture of something in the room where they are and work with everyone else to make an online photo collage. Then they have to explain the collage to the larger group. They can use anything from an app to Google slides to work together.
- **Make a class playlist:** This can be done in breakout rooms or as a larger group, but have the students make a list of songs they think fit the overall theme of the class. Choose one or two students to help organize a playlist on the music streaming platform of your choice. It will be fun and generate conversation around favorite songs and music choices. Keep the playlist and use it during class breaks. This builds community and collective, positive memories around the class and each other.
- **Class material hunt:** While the class will have its materials, engage the students in collecting other materials for bonus or alternative assignments. Send breakout rooms or groups of students on an Internet scavenger hunt to find videos, podcasts, blogs and other materials. Have them present their bounty to the class. Then have a vote about which items the students would like to have included in the course.

Again all of these keep the student centered while removing some of the pressure from the professor.

Finally, we also recommend "breaking out" of the breakout rooms and learning management systems by having class discussions in a variety of online spaces. Each generation has a favored gathering space. Now many of them are digital. Some are social media, gaming streams and apps meant for group communication. At the time of this book's publication, Twitch and Discord were two popular online gaming streams. In lieu of a regular class discussion, we organized a class game night and had casual chats and feedback sessions while playing. Students not interested in playing a particular game could join the stream and listen and comment.

Try something similar with office hours. Again, the space itself will depend upon tastes and trends, but rather than sitting in Zoom, have office hours in an app or conference platform. This enables people to drop in and out easily, is not dependent on a great internet connection and makes talking to groups easier. For example, Twitterspace or something similar allows for conversations and group posts. The professor can deal with multiple questions at the same time in a low-pressure environment. Clubhouse, HopIn and other conference applications revive the concept of a conference call. They allow one to cut back on screen time without losing engagement. Integrated graphics can be used to give the calls and spaces a certain appearance. The main benefit is ease of access and the sense of informality. Everyone can easily do these kinds of office hours from their phones without having to access any particular setup.

A note about these and all suggested activities concerning inclusion: be aware that not every student will have access to some tools. They may not have the best Internet connection or may be attending class from a location where they cannot show their surroundings. Be prepared to allow some students to not participate without fear of judgment. For issues where the institution can be helpful, such as connectivity, try to connect the students with those resources. In working to be engaged, it is important not to lose focus of being inclusive from a variety of perspectives.

Online learning does not have to be flat or two dimensional just because it is happening via a computer screen. Using collaboration tools and encouraging students to work together in teams and small groups, you can create an engaged online learning community.

III   I MISS THE CHALKBOARD, WHITEBOARD ETC.

This happens to many during the process of creating and teaching online classes. And while being student-centered is important in developing an inclusive, engaged learning community, the professor's need for comfort and variety cannot be overlooked. Just as some students prefer taking notes on paper over typing them in a computer or using a rocketbook per se, some of us just enjoy the "mind to hand" connection of the chalkboard. For the professor, the chalkboard is a means to organize thoughts. It can also be a discussion enhancer and makes reviewing easier. There are applications that mimic the sensation and muscle awareness of writing on a chalkboard. They can serve as a record of the conversation and memory booster in a similar fashion. You can also use these tools to generate debate and facilitate project-based learning.

The most obvious substitute for the whiteboard or chalkboard is using the whiteboard app. It works on multiple operating systems. The app allows you to write and display what you write in real time with students on Zoom, Teams and other meeting platforms. You can save the board and share it in your learning management system. One of its deficiencies is that it is not interactive. Using interactive boards achieves the ability to generate conversation and serve as a record of the conversation, but also allows students to do some of the writing and design. They have a range of functions. Google's Jamboard allows groups to make lists and share ideas on sticky notes that can then be organized and shared. Ziteboard allows collaborators to insert images, audio and has its own chat function that can all be saved along with the group's ideas on the board.

Canva and Mural take group collaboration beyond written ideas to multimedia and visual collaborations. In both, teams can design and even create art together. These are both great tools to use for arts and social media courses in lieu of being together in a lab or to enhance theory or history modules of related courses. For courses such as law, philosophy or other courses driven by argumentation there are discussion boards and ranking tools. Kialo is an example of a collaborative platform that allows all participants to put forth their ideas and then vote and rank them as the conversation proceeds. This is great for classes where narrowing the discussion or eliminating ideas during debate is a goal. It can also be used for planning and project design.

Other tools are uniquely useful for group projects. To help students communicate well and be able to get the most complete record of their communication and work, there are a few ways to accomplish the goal. Individual recordings can happen, but can also be difficult to manage in breakout rooms. For project-based learning, there are other platforms and applications that encourage idea sharing as writings, visualizations and even group recordings. At the time of writing, Flipgrid and Explain Everything are two tools being used in both classrooms and business environments. Flipgrid has conversation and project starters on a variety of topics to help initiate group work. Explain Everything has video messaging and the ability to bring all elements of the meeting together in one electronic brief. Depending on the configuration of your organization's learning management system, these tend to be compatible and can be linked with them. Alternatively, the work from these tools can be saved. Another more familiar tool that is often incorporated into systems is VoiceThread. One of the advantages of VoiceThread is that it is mobile-friendly. The tools mentioned here are examples pulled from dozens of currently available options with a focus on engagement and ease of use vis à vis traditional classroom tools.

Another staple of the classroom that is equally missed and reviled is the slide presentation. Both PowerPoint and Google Slides physically translate well to online environments. There are better tools available to make presentations easier to manage and are more interesting visually. These aspects can help with engagement and lessen the overwhelming impacts of online learning.

IV   AVOIDING "DEATH BY POWERPOINT" AND GOOGLE SLIDE OVERLOAD

These terms are almost a cliché, but not without reason. Many of us have a story of someone putting together dozens of text dense PowerPoint slides and then reading them to their audience. This kind of "presentation-based illiteracy" has exhausted audiences of all sizes since their creation. The phenomenon is not improved when done entirely online. As we learned from researchers at the University of Denver, the name for this is having a case of the "Zoombies" caused by being online for long periods of time (Toney et al., 2021). The reason for this particular kind of fatigue is that close up eye contact, even in an artificial environment, is tiring. That, partnered with seeing oneself for hours on end, creates a sense of arousal in the body. Add to that the "cognitive load" or amount of work our bodies have to do to understand visual and verbal cues and there is not much bandwidth left for a massive slideshow (Ramachandran, 2021). Toney, Light and Urbaczewski note that the antidote to the zoombies is activity switching, mixing up groups and changing how classwork is presented.

Part of the reason presentations can be so daunting for the audience is that people often use presentation tools as a crutch and center the conversation on the slides, rather than thinking of the presentation as a verbal performance and centering the focus on themselves and their subject matter expertise. Online spaces only amplify the differences between the former approach. The first step to better online presentations is to consider people, tools and time.

First, let's discuss tools. Part of engaging online learning is finding creative ways to challenge students. This definitely means eschewing presentation formats that are not the most exciting in real life, so they definitely don't translate well online. Teaching online presents a great opportunity to avoid "death by PowerPoint" and "Google slide overload". Mixing up presentation styles has multiple purposes. From a visual standpoint, it helps cut down on "Zoom fatigue" by giving students something different to look at and focus on, by changing the view of the screen. As a pedagogical technique, using tools is a layered learning opportunity. Students review and further internalize the course materials in order to create the presentations. They can use decision-making and editing skills. Also, there is an opportunity to expand their knowledge or digital fluency in selecting and learning how to use a new tool. There are a myriad of tools available, but each has its benefits and challenges depending on the professor's desire for student learning.

Next, try different presentation apps. For people who like the intuitiveness of PowerPoint, but hate the format limitations, Beautiful.ai is one alternative (Beautiful.ai, n.d.). It uses predictive analysis to help individuals and teams build presentations with unique, but consistent themes and the ability to check information as the project is created. Much to the disappointment of those who like eye contact and giving and receiving nonverbal feedback, the customary slide presentations tools cover most of the screen or move the presenter into a small section of the screen. The Mmhmm app allows for live online presentations in the style of a newscast. So the presenter not only stays on screen, but you can control how much of the screen is taken up by slides or other visuals.

Sometimes, just changing the style is what is needed for more appealing visuals. Prezi is probably one of the better-known options. It started as a slideshow with movement and a variety of formats to add the capacity to add music and embed videos. Now there is a flipped classroom function that allows for recording screencasts and other options. Pear Deck, ScreenCastify and Screen Cast-O-Matic are others with similar offerings. At their core, each of these improves the visual quality of the presentations and gives the creator more options for personalization.

For our consideration of people, think about the variety of learning styles amongst your students and consider how to present in a way that reaches as many of them as possible. Multimedia is a great way to go, as are interactive approaches. Students should consider the same with respect to their colleagues. Consider using props or other visual aids besides the presentation tool itself. As an example, try embedding a video or a photo essay into the presentation. Work with the students to create a storyboard. This can help tactile and auditory learners engage without isolating people who are more visually oriented.

You can also try different kinds of assignments for presentations. Slideshows do not have to be the default for presentations. Two other options are creating videos or photo essays. Many students who routinely use social media or are involved in creative arts will intuitively know how to create either of these. Almost all the platforms have a video creation function that is well used. There are also video editors and video makers on most smartphones. Videos offer students who may be introverted or not the most vocal in an open classroom another way to express themselves. The same is true for photo essays. Students are "trained" on how to create them from using apps like Instagram, but will benefit from applying the course subject matter to a new process. There is no need to introduce social media use into class, but it can serve as functional inspiration for the activity.

Storyboards can be used to turn assignments and presentations into personalized narratives. Storyboards are typically used in video and television production to help plan and organize plots. They are a roadmap from one point in the story to the next. In the classroom, storyboards can be used to help students track and organize main ideas and critical themes. They help with organizing historical timelines. In a presentation, storyboarding can help presenters conceptualize abstract ideas or lead the audience through complex arguments with the help of visual aids. Just as with video editors, there are a number of photo essays and storyboard applications that are easily downloaded for smartphone, tablet or computer use.

Finally, there is the consideration of time, specifically screen time. Be sure to balance slides and other visualizations with discussion and audio. A good rule of thumb is no more than 10–12 slides for each 30–45-minute-long presentation. For most people, this means about half of the time can be spent in discussion and engagement. It is also helpful to limit the number of presentations per class meeting and build in breaks. For an hour-long class meeting, no more than 30 minutes should be dedicated to presentations.

Besides diversifying presentation options, students and professors can benefit from encouraging alternatives to essays and capstone theses as

Table 7.1   Animation and storyboard applications

Boords: https://boords.com	Storyboard and animatics, good for teams and group projects, free resource
Storyboard That: https://www.storyboardthat .com	Canvas and Google friendly, can be adapted for accessibility, free resource
Glogster: http://edu.glogster.com/?ref=com	Multimedia poster creator, can also create lecture notes with visualizations
Powtoon: Video Maker: https://www.powtoon .com/	Video and visual communication creator, Canvas friendly

assignments. Table 7.1 provides some examples of applications that can be used for some of these kinds of assignments.

Noting that technology changes rapidly, these are examples from a crowded field of online learning tools and LMS add-ons. These are based on personal experience and ease of use for both the instructor and students. They also work with accessibility tools and have offline modes for when there are Internet accessibility issues. The final factor was cost. Knowing that university budgets vary, a priority was placed on free and low-cost options. I share both the tools and the approach to selecting them to help with future tool selection decisions.

V   ASSIGN SOMETHING OTHER THAN CAPSTONE THESES OR ESSAYS

Assigning something other than academic journal articles and journalism as readings exposes students to different formats, ideas and experiences. Giving assignments of different formats adds variety to the course structure, but also challenges students' ability to evaluate different kinds of materials. From a pedagogical perspective, it is important to continuously evaluate the nature of student learning and seek opportunities to expand it, often with the students' involvement (Felten, 2013).

Thinking about the consequences of assignment choices on the student experience is of value in all classroom settings, even online classrooms. This approach is a feature of the Scholarship of Teaching and Learning as well as the theory of Teaching As Commons. This seeks to end the "solitude" of scholarship and learning by treating the process as community property. There is also a proposal to attach teaching styles more closely to the discipline being taught (Shulman, 1993). What these approaches confirm is that innovation and connection are important components of engagement and community. Innovation can take many forms, here it can be thoughtfulness with respect to assignments and evaluation.

Journal articles and journalism as reading assignments challenge critical thinking and evaluation. Assigning similar tasks, such as essay writing, tests similar skills. But there should also be opportunities to challenge one's thinking, incorporate logic or even add visual and non-linear expressions of understanding. Podcasts, YouTube videos and mini documentaries are great assignments that add this nonlinear element. Because they are often found in digital common spaces and communities, using them in lieu of reading or assigning them to be created by students allows them to access other communities beyond the classroom. This not only generates internal interest, but is part of the development of digital literacy and citizenship discussed earlier. It allows them to be co-creators of material inside and outside of the classroom.

Preparing students for digital citizenship and life outside the classroom lends itself to more practical writing assignments. This is an opportunity to be creative and discipline specific. Law students can be encouraged to write legal briefs or case notes as they would in a law firm or for a judge. Students interested in policy might benefit from writing a draft bill, policy statement or Op-Eds. Public health or health-related fields could have a patient assessment or set of operational principles as assignments. The idea is to give them an experiential opportunity. This will enhance classroom learning but also encourage career preparation and engagement in the discipline in which the class is centered. In addition to other kinds of guest speakers, consider a speaker and evaluator. For example, in an undergraduate political science class, the students who wrote a draft bill had an opportunity to discuss it with a legislative staffer who guest lectured on the legislative topic during the same class. The students were able to benefit from the real-world experience of the staffer combined with feedback from the instructor.

Changing the way students learn brings new skills to bear such as discerning the validity and applicability of information, a skill that comes with frequent use of online resources. That said, a constant challenge in higher education generally is fairly assessing students' progress. With online learning and alternative assignments, that can be more difficult. Traditional rubrics may not fit exactly, so creative thinking about assessments or even creating new rubrics is needed. Admittedly, this can be time consuming. Another approach is to work with campus resources such as academic affairs, teaching and learner centers and disability services to consider ways of adapting existing rubrics. In all, it is a balance of time versus the long-term goals of your course design approach.

If you decide to incorporate alternative assessments as part of your alternative assignment approach, there are interesting and even fulfilling ways to do it. First, remember the goal of assignments and assessments is to understand what students can accomplish with what they are learning, not how well they have memorized the materials. Think of framing assessments to focus on what students can do as much as what they know (Ryerson University, n.d.). If you decide to create a rubric, consider basing it on outcomes rather than processes. Essentially, asking for demonstration of learning over test taking abilities is a good approach for rubrics associated with alternative assignments. Some universities and school systems offer rubric sets that contemplate a variety of assignments. It is likely that you will need to create a specific rubric set for your class or a bespoke evaluation framework. For the rubric, most learning management systems have a rubric creation function. For the framework, you can incorporate it into your class sections or modules. Another option is to make it part of your syllabus. In any circumstance the key is to make sure the evaluation standards are clearly communicated to students.

The first step is to ask yourself a series of questions:

- What are the core skills students need to take from this class?
- What am I testing or evaluating with this assignment?
- How do the assignment and the goals I identified relate to the core skills and focus of the class?

Using this approach will result in an assessment process that allows students to demonstrate their abilities, their understanding and develop an ability to receive competency-based feedback. Create a list, chart or image of what it looks like for an assignment, the core skills you aim to teach with it and the competency as an outcome to converge. Then make a list of competencies, such as: critical reflection, reasoning, argumentation, problem solving, writing, conceptualizing, collaboration, creativity, civic and global learning and digital literacy. For each assignment, create a rubric or framework that combines the core skills, or answers to your questions, with a competency from the list you created.

Here is an example using some of the practical assignments mentioned before:

Table 7.2   *Skills and assessment chart*

Assignment	Core skills	Competency
Patient Assessment	Communications Evaluation skills	Problem solving Collaboration Critical thinking
Policy Brief	Systems-based thinking Understanding dense materials	Reasoning Critical reflection Writing
Mini-documentary	Understanding complex concepts Distillation of multiple forms of information	Creativity Civic or global learning Conceptualization

These assignments accomplish the engagement goals of almost any class. Additionally, thinking about the learning outcomes and expectations provides a consistent grading framework upon which the instructor and student can rely. Another key component of engagement that allows consistent outcomes and grading is the ability to conduct research successfully in an online environment. One way to address this is by incorporating research guides into the course.

REFERENCES

Arhin, A. O., & Johnson-Mallard, V. (2003). "Encouraging alternative forms of self expression in the generation Y student: A strategy for effective learning in the classroom". *ABNF Journal*, 14(6), pp. 121+. *Gale Academic OneFile*, accessed 28 June 2021.

Awidi, I. T., & Paynter, M. (2019). "The impact of a flipped classroom approach on student learning experience". *Computers & Education*, 128, pp. 269–83, ISSN 0360-1315. Available at: https://www.sciencedirect.com/science/article/pii/S0360131518302495.

Beautiful.ai. (n.d.). Presentation Maker: From Basic to Beautiful in Minutes with Beautiful.ai. Available at: https://www.beautiful.ai/.

Digital Fluency in the Classroom. (n.d.). *Digital Fluency in the Classroom.* Available at: https://digitalfluencyintheclassroom.weebly.com/; https://www.digitallearningcollab.com/blog/what-is-digital-fluency.

Felten, P. (2013). "Principles of good practice in SoTL". *Teaching & Learning Inquiry: The ISSOTL Journal*, 1(1), pp. 121–25. Available at: doi:10.2979/teachlearninqu.1.1.121.

Jukes, I. (2015). Global Digital Citizen Foundation. 21st Century Fluencies. Retrieved from: https://globaldigitalcitizen.org/21st-century-fluencies.

Ramachandran, V. (2021). "Stanford researchers identify four causes for 'zoom fatigue' and their simple fixes". *Stanford News*, 23 February. Available at: https://news.stanford.edu/2021/02/23/four-causes-zoom-fatigue-solutions/.

Ribble, M., & Bailey, G. D. (2007). *Digital Citizenship in Schools*. International Society for Technology in Education.

Ryerson University. (n.d.). *Best Practices: Alternative Assessments*. Available at: https://www.ryerson.ca/content/dam/learning-teaching/teaching-resources/assessment/alternative-assessments.pdf.

Shulman, L. S. (1993). "Teaching as community property; putting an end to pedagogical solitude". *Change*, Nov–Dec 25(6), p6(2). Available at: http://depts.washington.edu/comgrnd/ccli/papers/shulman1993TeachingAsCommunityProperty.pdf.

Toney, S., Light, J., & Urbaczewski, A. (2021). "Fighting zoom fatigue: Keeping the zoombies at bay". *Communications of the Association for Information Systems*, 48. Available at: https://doi.org/10.17705/1CAIS.04806.

8. Developing and incorporating impactful library research guides for online and hybrid learners

Ladislava Khailova

An aspect of online and hybrid course design that may occasionally get overlooked by instructional designers and faculty alike due to disciplinary boundaries involves ensuring that students understand how to fully take advantage of the institution's library research resources. Yet, as scholarly literature documents, when classes are online and the physical contact with the library in the traditional sense is not present, students can easily miss out on the benefits that library offerings have for their academic experience (Gonzalez & Westbrock, 2010). The issue can become exacerbated if the online classes are taught by part-time faculty members who themselves may not have had a chance to become thoroughly familiar with the specific library's collections and other assets (Clever, 2020). In situations like these, students are prone to rush to Google for their research needs (Adebonojo, 2010), often overlooking the higher-quality proprietary aggregates of electronic and digitizable print resources their library provides to them without the Google-like full-text access paywalls. Along the same lines, they may fail to utilize the expert assistance librarians can offer to them when trying to effectively evaluate and use the sources they retrieve for their research projects (Adebonojo, 2010).

For several decades now, academic librarians, frequently aided by faculty, have been trying to address this less than optimal situation by developing online library research guides that explicitly try to connect online and hybrid students to the library resources and services that can help them succeed. Generally, these guides take many forms, from subject guides that provide access to a curated set of resources for a certain discipline, to course or assignment guides that assist students with specific course work, to library orientation guides that answer common questions about library offerings or policies (Conerton &

Goldenstein, 2017). In their multiplicity, the guides can play a significant role in attempting to fill any gap caused by the online learners not being physically present on campus to interact with the library and its staff in-person and/or synchronously. The purpose of this chapter is to outline strategies educators can utilize to enhance the impact of these library research guides for the purposes of student-centered, inclusive, and accessible online learning and research. More specifically, the chapter discusses the importance of faculty actively contributing to the creation and dissemination of library research guides, including following best practices for effective and accessible guide design and understanding options for guide incorporation in Learning Management Systems (LMS) as well as related course e-materials.

## I	BENEFITS OF FACULTY CONTRIBUTING TO LIBRARY RESEARCH GUIDES

While by the default definition of library research guides, librarians tend to be the main driving force behind the creation and distribution of these digital learning objects, direct input from faculty substantially impacts the success rate of the guides. In more detail, online library guides that are developed or edited in collaboration with the course or program faculty consistently show the greatest levels of use by students (Adebonojo, 2010; Clever, 2020; Gonzalez & Westbrock, 2010). For example, as Adebonojo (2010) reports, when public services librarians at the East Tennessee State University's Sherrod Library determined that it would be beneficial to create an online library research guide for each of the classes they taught a library information literacy session for, they gave the faculty the power to make a decision about the depth to which library resources would be presented on their course guides. As a result, the guides showed a higher than usual level of utilization by students (Adebonojo, 2010). This observation is not surprising, considering that faculty as subject experts have intimate knowledge of not only the targeted discipline, but also the specific content of the courses taught within this discipline by the educational institution. Correspondingly, they prove to serve as invaluable partners for librarians when compiling a list of high-quality library resources and related instructional materials that students in online or hybrid courses should engage with. At the same time, the partnership does not have to be overwhelming for faculty. Even when faculty provide input at a "casual level", as represented, for example, by them simply reviewing the finished library research guides and making suggestions for possible additional enhancements, the guide usage numbers are prone to be high (Clever, 2020, p. 50). Ultimately, it is the librarian-faculty collaboration towards the common goal of impactful, inclusive library research guides that makes all the difference.

II   LIBGUIDES AS A PREFERRED SOFTWARE CHOICE FOR LIBRARY RESEARCH GUIDES

While the market provides several software packages that can help librarian-faculty collaborators design and implement effective library research guides, LibGuides continues to serve as the preferred platform for most academic institutions (Fagerheim et al., 2017). Defined by Springshare (2020), its creating company, as "an easy-to-use content management system", LibGuides has a tabbed interface, and offers a combination of columns and boxes that allow guide creators to fairly quickly compile visually appealing curated collections of readily accessible library research resources, such as relevant article databases, online journals, ebooks, and datasets that the institution subscribes to and provides free of charge to the institution's learners. Embedding associated pedagogical materials that aid the learners in conducting research (e.g., video tutorials) is also easy within LibGuides. Additionally, the platform contains comparatively advanced built-in features that complement such embedding, including a broken link checker, a librarian profile creator, and a blogging option. LibGuides' reporting capabilities are quite powerful as well, enabling guide compilers to receive statistics reflecting the learner usage of their individual guides. At the same time, the utilization of LibGuides for library research guide creation does not require any prior experience with web design or HTML, making it appealing to faculty and librarians across the programming skills spectrum (Gonzalez & Westbrock, 2010).

In accordance with the listed advantages, the LibGuides community continues to grow. While in 2012, Springshare reported having approximately 3,125 library customers who developed over 248,000 research guides (Sonsteby & DeJonghe, 2013), in 2020, it disclosed having "thousands of libraries worldwide" that have collectively created over 500,000 guides available within the LibGuides community for sharing and reuse (Springshare, 2020). The numbers are only expected to keep rising.

To present an example of an online library research guide created using the LibGuides platform, Figure 8.1 below displays a portion of the home page of a subject guide developed by this chapter's author for the Supply

Chain Management Master of Professional Studies (MPS) Program at Georgetown University's (GU) School of Continuing Studies (SCS). The subject guide contains several box types used consistently across the SCS Library's LibGuides research guides, such as a brief welcome, a librarian profile with a link to the research consultation scheduler, and a list of core links featuring easily accessible databases most relevant for the program. As is also the custom for the SCS Library, the tabs within the guide organize the included high-profile library resources by both format and topic area in order to cater to a wide range of SCS Supply Chain Management students' information needs.

III   RECOMMENDED BEST PRACTICES FOR DEVELOPING EFFECTIVE ONLINE LIBRARY RESEARCH GUIDES

The LibGuides library research guide example from Figure 8.1 leads us to consider the best practices librarian-faculty collaborators should follow when aiming to develop highly impactful guides. Existing evidence-based scholarship on the topic of LibGuides provides helpful guidance along the way, with suggestions focusing on the broader categories of guide layout and design as well as content.

A   Best Practices for Library Research Guide Layout and Design

To begin with guide layout and design, an interesting debate exists on the issue of the most effective scope of online library research guides. A strong strain of the LibGuides scholarship recommends that creators aim at developing guides that are course-specific or assignment-specific rather than generic, tying the argument to the results of usability studies and relevant usage statistics (Adebonojo, 2010; Conerton & Goldenstein, 2017; Gonzalez & Westbrock, 2010). For instance, librarians at New Mexico State University conclude that the library research guide they developed to help undergraduate students with a particular business class assignment received more hits during one semester than all of their more general guides combined (Gonzalez & Westbrock, 2010). That said, another strain of the studies provides a counter-argument: it asserts that broader-scope guides, as represented in this chapter by the example of the GU SCS Supply Chain Management MPS program-focused guide from Figure 8.1, are the ones most utilized by students. Thus, Murphy

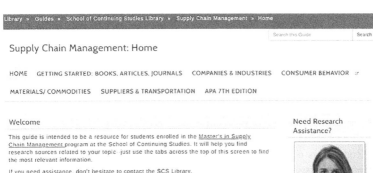

*Figure 8.1   GU SCS Library LibGuide for the SCS Supply Chain
Management MPS Program*

and Black (2013) document that almost all of the high-use guides at the
Ohio State University were created at the department or college level,
with the course-level guides instead accounting for more than 68%
of the lowest-performing pages. Contradictions like these likely stem
from learners' preferences varying widely when it comes to the breadth
of information they expect to see within a library research guide, with

the preference closely dependent on their immediate information need (Conerton & Goldenstein, 2017). Therefore, to satisfy the full scale of online and hybrid student research needs, librarian and faculty collaborators are advised to offer a mixture of subject-/discipline-specific as well as course-/assignment-specific library research guides within their institution. As a reminder, it is crucial for faculty to be quite vocal during this stage of the guide conceptualization process, using their knowledge of the targeted student population as well as of the discipline to help drive decisions about the guide scope for any given online or hybrid class.

Regardless of the resulting scope, creators should plan for the guide design to be streamlined and visually consistent. Within LibGuides, the key is to strategically limit the number of tabs, aiming at including only the most pertinent ones. Numerically, this recommendation often translates into the library research guides having seven or fewer tabs (Goodsett et al., 2020; Sonsteby & DeJonghe, 2013). The tabs ought to be named in a consistent fashion and presented within similar places on research guides. Additionally, the content within the individual tabs should be carefully segmented to prevent student cognitive overload, making the affected pages and boxes short and easy to scroll through (Conerton & Goldenstein, 2017; Goodsett et al., 2020). The use of advanced text segmenting principles, such as columns, bullets, or headings, is also encouraged, with the segmentation features repeated across guides, and text fonts, color schemes, and backgrounds in general matching as well (Conerton & Goldenstein, 2017; Goodsett et al., 2020).

Additionally, the streamlined, visually consistent guide content should be organized hierarchically to make it easier for online students to quickly identify and access those library resources that are most relevant to them. Correspondingly, instead of using the alphabet to arrange any lists of featured research resources (such as databases, datasets, and books), librarians and faculty should aim to introduce these resources to students in the order of their significance (Goodsett et al., 2020; Sonsteby & DeJonghe, 2013). For online and hybrid courses, basing the significance at least partially on the ease with which students can access the resources is a key. For instance, full-text online resources that allow for an unlimited number of concurrent users should be noticeably prioritized over resources that may have wait times associated with them due to licensing caps on simultaneous users, or that require a trip to the physical library. Taking these suggestions one step further, it is recommended that the most impactful of these resources be highlighted via a prominently placed tab or box labeled Core Links, Key Resources, Best Bets, or the like (Goodsett et al., 2020).

B   Best Practices for Library Research Guide Content

Similarly to layout and design, the library research guide content also comes with its related set of effectiveness-boosting best practices. In fact, the issue of tab naming overlaps with the topic of the overall use of language in research guides. More specifically, less-than-optimal use of terminology in guides has been repeatedly identified by researchers in usability studies as one of the leading obstacles preventing students from successfully completing assigned research tasks (Conerton & Goldenstein, 2017; Sonsteby & DeJonghe, 2013). Students seem to particularly struggle with jargon, represented by librarians using words that do not match student understanding of what they are looking for. For instance, librarians and students tend to hold divergent definitions of such key terms as "reference sources" or even "databases" (Sonsteby & DeJonghe, 2013). Faculty as non-librarians can provide valuable input here, helping to pinpoint any jargon-heavy labels for guide tabs, boxes, menus, or pages that might be potentially misinterpreted by users. Along the same lines, faculty can assist librarians in coming up with meaningful alternatives for these labels, such as the more descriptive "encyclopedias/ handbooks" term for reference sources, or "article databases" or "journal articles" for the potentially more obscure term "databases". In cases when the alternative labels may still not be self-explanatory, faculty and librarians can collaboratively draft accompanying annotations to relay the intended meaning more clearly to learners (Goodsett et al., 2020).

While providing verbal explanations within online guides is often helpful, guide creators should make sure that their products also incorporate multimedia content to maximize student learning. Since the guides, particularly in the form of LibGuides, have initially evolved from paper handouts or pathfinders (Gonzalez & Westbrock, 2010), it may be tempting to think of them primarily as a rather text-based medium. However, due to the rapid developments in digital learning technologies, current students rightfully expect a higher level of dynamism and interactivity from the online guides than their predecessors may have a few decades ago. These expectations match Gagne's argument that using visually presented information is an effective means of gaining students' attention, with the human brain known to respond to such information fast (UF Center for Instructional Technology and Training, n.d.). Accordingly, it is essential for librarian and faculty guide collaborators to aim to incorporate pedagogical audiovisual resources, such as brief video tutorials on key aspects of conducting online research.

Even with the most learning-material rich guides, students may have follow-up questions at some point in the research process. To that end, it is recommended to include a creator profile box in the guide (Goodsett et al., 2020). Within LibGuides, the profile box typically features the librarian: more specifically, the librarian professional photo, their contact information, and, where available, a link for scheduling a research consultation or chatting live with them. The presence of the profile box is especially crucial within the possibly isolating online learning environment, personalizing the digital guide for the learners and emphasizing to them that they are not left to their own devices: rather, there is a dedicated research specialist available to them within a few clicks.

Under ideal circumstances, the proposed guide layout and design as well as content best practices are applied consistently across the institution's library research guides. Students are known to thrive in online environments that offer reliable patterns aiding their cognitive processing of information. When such uniformity and predictability is lacking in guides, students tend to notice it and become overwhelmed (Fagerheim et al., 2017; Sonsteby & DeJonghe, 2013). To prevent this from happening and assist guide collaborators in achieving the desired level of uniformity as well as to save their time, academic institutions should consider creating a template or master guide that can be flexibly adopted by all (Gonzalez & Westbrock, 2010; Goodsett et al., 2020).

For the purposes of helping institutions with the development of such a template, the covered best practices for library research guide creation are summarized in the checklist below, with special focus on the LibGuides platform. Essential guide accessibility requirements are not included here as they are discussed in detail in the chapter's next section, with a separate library research guide accessibility checklist to follow.

BOX 8.1   LIBRARY RESEARCH GUIDE LAYOUT/ DESIGN AND CONTENT BEST PRACTICES CHECKLIST[1]

[1] The Library Research Guide Layout/Design and Content Best Practices Checklist should be used in conjunction with the Library Research Guide Accessibility Checklist (Box 8.2).

Layout and design

- Scope Variation
  - A combination of discipline-/subject-level and course-/ assignment-level library research guides is offered by the institution.
- Streamlining
  - Only the most pertinent tabs are included (preferably, seven or fewer tabs total).
  - Each guide is broken down into meaningful sections, resulting in short pages/boxes.
- Visual Consistency
  - Key tabs have consistent labels and appear in similar places across guides.
  - Guide style and design (fonts, colors, background, etc.) match from guide to guide.
- Hierarchical Organization
  - Resources are organized by importance rather than alphabetically or numerically.
  - Easy-access e-resources (especially those allowing for an unlimited number of concurrent users) are featured prominently within each guide.
  - The guides contain a "Core List," "Key Resources," or "Best Bets" tab or box.

Content

- Language
  - Unnecessary jargon, including acronyms, is left out.
  - Tools/resources under tabs and boxes that may not be self-explanatory are accompanied by annotations.
- Multimedia
  - Text-based information is supplemented by audiovisual materials, such as video tutorials.
- Librarian/Faculty Presence
  - The guides feature a librarian/faculty profile box with contact information.
- Template/Master Guide
  - A template/master guide is available to all guide creators.

IV   LIBRARY RESEARCH GUIDE ACCESSIBILITY REQUIREMENTS

As mentioned above, online library research guide creation also comes with its specific set of accessibility legal requirements and moral obligations. According to the Centers for Disease and Control Prevention (2020), the number of U.S. adults who self-identify as having a disability is quite substantial: there are approximately 61 million (or one in four) such adults in the United States. Their rights to full and equal access are most significantly protected under the Americans with Disabilities Act of 1990 (Hopper, 2021). When it comes to equal access to web-based content, such as library research guides, users who are blind or have serious difficulties seeing are at especially high risk of coming across discriminatory barriers. Accordingly, available scholarship on the accessible design of LibGuides and related guide software discusses primarily the issue of guide readability by screen readers (e.g., JAWS or ZoomText) that have the capability of converting the online guide text and image content into speech and/or Braille. That said, since guide users with hearing impairments can also potentially be negatively impacted by digital presentation of content, a smaller portion of the literature provides guidelines for the accessibility of hearing-dependent library research guide elements (e.g., multimedia). The sections below divide the related guide accessibility requirements into categories mimicking the structure of the broader best practices for library research guide creation, i.e., layout and design and content.

A   Library Research Guide Layout and Design Accessibility Requirements

In terms of the overall layout and design of library research guides, guide creators should utilize built-in features within LibGuides to organize the content. For example, rather than using large font sizes or putting text in bold to distinguish between sections, librarian and faculty collaborators are advised to make use of the heading options within the LibGuides' Rich Text Editor. Headings play an essential role in allowing readers with visual impairments to quickly select the parts of the text that they want to read as screen readers will typically read out the headings to them first (GW Libraries, 2020). While LibGuides allow for heading levels 1 through 6, heading 1 is typically reserved for LibGuides' titles and heading 2 for LibGuides' box titles. Accordingly, guide creators should structure their text hierarchically under headings 3 to 6 (GW Libraries, 2020). Similarly, lists and tables should also be created using LibGuides built-in options when organizing information, with the specification that tables be employed for data presentation only (as opposed to general layout) and contain row/column headers and captions (CUNY, 2021).

To ensure an optimal learning experience by all, the guides additionally need to employ accessible color schemes. While color can enhance information processing, it is imperative that guide creators do not rely on color alone to convey meaning since that information will generally not be available to learners who use screen readers or are color blind (WebAIM, 2021b). In fact, all of the guides' presentation of text as well as images of text needs to meet established foreground and background color contrast requirements to make the guide compliant. To that end, librarians and faculty are encouraged to run the guides through such authoritative tools as the WebAIM Contrast Checker prior to making them available to online classes (WebAIM, 2021a).

B   Library Research Guide Content Accessibility Requirements

Moving on to aspects specific to the library research guide content, hyperlinks deserve special attention since their incorporation often leads to violations of accessible practices. To that end, GW Libraries (2020) emphasize that guide creators need to aim at crafting hyperlink text that is specific to the extent that it is meaningful on its own. Therefore, hyperlinks should never be simply directional (e.g., "Click this link") as online learners would not be able to take full advantage of them without actually acting on the directional command. Likewise, hyperlinks should not contain the link address itself (e.g., see www.library.georgetown.edu/ scs) as a screen reader would read out loud every letter and symbol within it, making the text of the link generally incomprehensible (GW Libraries, 2020). In applying these principles, a sample inaccessible link in the form of "Schedule an appointment here" could thus be revised to an accessible link stating, "To schedule an appointment, use our consultation booking system".

In relation to images as another key content element of the guides, the accessibility mandate is to make them "visible" to users of screen readers by accompanying them with adequate alternative text or, for short, alt text (CUNY, 2021). When images have no alt text, screen readers tend to skip them or read the file name of the image instead (e.g., IMB345.jpg), making learners with visual impairments miss out on the information that these images try to convey. Along these lines, images with unhelpful alt text also result in losses in content comprehension. Therefore, it is recommended that guide creators provide a specific yet succinct image description of five or more words, while simultaneously leaving out redundant phrases signaling the presence of an image (e.g., "the picture of") since the use of alt text already fulfills that function (GW Libraries, 2020). Using the image from the home page of the GU SCS Supply Chain Management MPS program library research guide from Figure 8.1 as an example, the alt text could thus read "A supply chain as represented by a truck and airplane passing through a storage area filled with large metal shipping containers."

Multimedia, including videos, come with their own set of accessibility requirements, this time linked rather to their possibly heavy dependence on the spoken word. To assist those who have trouble hearing or processing oral language, the use of multimedia stipulates the provision of closed captions and downloadable transcripts that translate the spoken word into text. Prominent video conferencing software packages (e.g., Zoom) and video sharing platforms (e.g., YouTube) will often help with this requirement by auto-generating the needed captions and/or transcripts. However, library research guide creators are always advised to carefully check these for accuracy and make any necessary edits before sharing them with classes. As GU's Center for New Designs in Learning and Scholarship (2021) insightfully observes, providing accurate captions and transcripts has the added benefit of assisting groups without disabilities as well: for instance, students who watch the guides' instructional videos in their non-native language and/or those whose internet bandwidth does not allow for an optimal video viewing experience will also likely find the assistive text useful. Similarly helpful to many groups of learners can be adding video titles. Accordingly, when embedding multimedia via LibGuides' iFrame – an html element used to display the media on the LibGuides page – guide creators need to remember to provide a title allowing users of all abilities to understand what object they have encountered (GW Libraries, 2020).

Since the outlined guide accessibility requirements may seem rather complex at times, the checklist below breaks them down into smaller, more specific, and manageable tasks. In order to ensure compliance, library research guide creators should be able to checkmark all of the listed items before publishing their guides.

BOX 8.2   LIBRARY RESEARCH GUIDE ACCESSIBILITY CHECKLIST

Layout and design

- Headings
  - The guide uses headings (rather than font-based differentiators such as size) to visually break the text into sections and/or subsections.
  - Higher level headings are placed above lower level headings to create a hierarchical progression.
  - In-text headings begin at heading level 3.
- Lists and Tables
  - Lists and tables are created using built-in formatting rather than manually.
  - The guide uses tables for data presentation only.
  - All tables have headers.
  - All tables contain a caption.
- Color Scheme
  - No part of the guide aims to convey meaning through color alone.
  - Visual presentation of text meets foreground and background color contrast requirements as confirmed by the WebAIM Contrast Checker.

Content

- Hyperlinks
  - All hyperlinks are descriptive and meaningful when read out of context.
  - There are no URL addresses included directly within the text of hyperlinks.
- Images
  - All images have alt text clearly describing the image without using phrases such as an "image of" or "picture of".
- Multimedia/Videos
  - All included multimedia/videos contain accurate closed-captioning.
  - All included multimedia/videos are accompanied by error-free transcripts.
  - IFrames of embedded multimedia/videos contain a title.

V INTEGRATING LIBRARY RESEARCH GUIDES IN LMS AND OTHER COURSE E-MATERIALS

To make it easier for online and hybrid learners to locate and utilize the carefully designed, accessible library research guides while working on their research assignments, the institution needs to have an effective plan for increasing the guide visibility. Similar to the guide creation process, faculty play a key role here. More closely, while most institutions advertise any existing library research guides within the library websites, studies show that the guides are likely to be more impactful when they are also incorporated in the faculty's course Learning Management System (e.g., Canvas or Blackboard) and other course e-materials (e.g., syllabi or assignments), with the faculty helping to facilitate and/or promote such embedding (Fagerheim et al., 2017). After all, online learners rely heavily on LMS and the course materials posted within them to gain access to course-pertinent information and to complete their coursework. Having matching library research guide(s) incorporated right in these environments increases the likelihood of the online learners coming across the library's curated collections of accessible resources and services and perceiving them as vetted. Since LMS tend to act as a gateway to other course e-materials, they are addressed here first, with the possibility of LibGuides based library research guides being linked within them either manually or automatically.

In terms of manually incorporating library research guides in LMS, the process is quite straightforward, and consists of inserting the permanent link to the guide(s) in the desired location within LMS – for example, under a navigation option labelled Library, Library Research Guide, Research Help, and the like. Either the faculty member or the librarian can complete the linking task, with the important reminder that if faculty prefer for a librarian to be in charge of the related steps, they need to add them to their course's LMS and grant them course content editing privileges. Such manual guide integration within LMS can represent a viable option especially in situations when the personnel face expertise challenges making it difficult for them to automate the linking action (Clever, 2020). That said, embedding a substantial amount of library research guides within an institution's LMS by hand can also be perceived as too burdensome and/or time-consuming by librarians and faculty, and ultimately be found unsustainable by them (Fagerheim et al., 2017).

Correspondingly, many institutions opt to automate the guide integration process. In relation to LibGuides, the step is generally accomplished by utilizing Springshare's LibApps Learning Tools Interoperability (LTI) protocol (Clever, 2020). Given the computer programming requirements associated with the use of LTI, cooperation among units is often vital. For instance, as Fagerheim et al. (2017) describe, at Utah State University, librarians collaborated with the University Center for Innovative Design and Instruction to build an LTI tool that automatically selects the most relevant library research guide for each Canvas course. The tool does so by matching the coded information librarians provided about each published LibGuide within the guide's description field with the Canvas data available for the courses. In cases when the LTI tool cannot identify a course or subject research guide match for a specific Canvas course, a generic library research guide is chosen (Fagerheim et al., 2017).

The impact of embedding library research guides in LMS, whether automated or manual, is further enhanced by a simultaneous incorporation of the guide links in additional course e-materials, such as syllabi or individual assignments – particularly if these assignments contain a research component. In these cases, due to document ownership issues, faculty generally need to act as the implementers of the guide links, but can always receive assistance from librarians in relation to the guide selection process. While the resulting embedding of guides in both LMS and e-syllabi/e-assignments may seem duplicative, it is highly likely to result in tangible benefits for the online learners. As research shows, linking library research guides directly within various online course materials is an effective way for helping students with those information needs that they find most challenging (Murphy & Black, 2013). Students being presented with multiple points of entry to these guides through the repeated linking process then increases the probability of them locating the guides at their highest point of need, taking full advantage of the guides' offerings.

VI   CONCLUSION

As highlighted in this chapter, when faculty join forces with librarians and collaborate on developing and incorporating inclusive library research guides for online and hybrid courses, the guides carry a strong potential for playing a pivotal role in the academic experience of the learners. Conceived of as a compilation of carefully selected high-quality, easily accessible library resources and services, the guides remind the learners that the library and its dedicated personnel are just a click away, helping to reduce any sense of disconnectedness they may experience due to the more challenging aspects of the online and hybrid course environments.

Perhaps more importantly, the guides clearly communicate to the learners that they do not need to rely on largely unvetted and paywalls-blocked online sources offered through such search engines as Google since the online library offers more viable alternatives. The guides can thus help instill quality in student research products, potentially also contributing to favorable course and program completion rates. In view of these combined benefits, library research guides deserve to be given close attention during any online or hybrid course development, with faculty continuing to serve as their highly desirable co-creators and co-marketers.

REFERENCES

Adebonojo, L. G. (2010). "LibGuides: Customizing subject guides for individual courses". *College & Undergraduate Libraries*, 17(4), pp. 398–412. Available at: https://doi.org/10.1080/10691316.2010.525426.

Center for New Designs in Learning and Scholarship. (2021). *Accessibility in Virtual Learning Environments*. Georgetown University. Available at: https://instructionalcontinuity.georgetown.edu/accessibility-2/#_ga=2.195157932 .1099206096.1606092453-676118085.1597024160.

Centers for Disease Control and Prevention. (2020). *Disability Impacts All of Us*. Available at: https://www.cdc.gov/ncbddd/disabilityandhealth/infographic -disability-impacts-all.html.

Clever, K. A. (2020). "Connecting with faculty and students through course-related LibGuides". *Pennsylvania Libraries: Research & Practice*, 8(1), pp. 49–57. Available at: https://doi.org/10.5195/palrap.2020.215.

Conerton, K., & Goldenstein, C. (2017). "Making LibGuides work: Student interviews and usability tests". *Internet Reference Services Quarterly*, 22(1), pp. 43–54. Available at: https://doi.org/10.1080/10875301.2017.1290002.

CUNY. (2021). *Accessibility Toolkit for Open Educational Resources (OER): LibGuides (Springshare)*. Available at: https://guides.cuny.edu/accessibility/ libguides.

Fagerheim, B., Lundstrom, K., Davis, E., & Cochran, D. (2017). "Extending our reach: Automatic integration of course and subject guides". *Reference & User Services Quarterly*, 56(3), pp. 180–88. Available at: https://doi.org/10.5860/ rusq.56n3.180.

Gonzalez, A. C., & Westbrock, T. (2010). "Reaching out with LibGuides: Establishing a working set of best practices". *Journal of Library Administration*, 50, pp. 638–56. Available at: https://doi.org/10.1080/01930826.2010.488941.

Goodsett, M., Miles, M., & Nawalaniec, T. (2020). "Reimagining research guidance: Using a comprehensive literature review to establish best practices for developing LibGuides". *Evidence Based Library and Information Practice*, 15(1), pp. 218–25. Available at: https://doi.org/10.18438/eblip29679.

GW Libraries. (2020). *Creating Accessible LibGuides.* Available at: https://libguides.gwu.edu/c.php?g=1000325.

Hopper, T. L. (2021). "Accessibility and LibGuides in academic libraries". *The Southeastern Librarian*, 68(4), pp. 12–28.

Murphy, S. A., & Black, E. L. (2013). "Embedding guides where students learn: Do design choices and librarian behavior make a difference?". *The Journal of Academic Librarianship*, 39(6), pp. 528–34. Available at: https://doi.org/10.1016/j.acalib.2013.06.007.

Sonsteby, A., & DeJonghe, J. (2013). "Usability testing, user-centered design, and LibGuides subject guides: A case study". *Journal of Web Librarianship*, 7(1), pp. 83–94. Available at: https://doi.org/10.1080/19322909.2013.747366.

Springshare. (2020). *LibGuides.* Available at: https://www.springshare.com/libguides/.

UF Center for Instructional Technology and Training. (n.d.). *Gagne's 9 Events of Instruction.* University of Florida. Available at: https://citt.ufl.edu/resources/the-learning-process/designing-the-learning-experience/gagnes-9-events-of-instruction/.

WebAIM. (2021a). *Contrast Checker.* Available at: https://webaim.org/resources/contrastchecker/.

WebAIM. (2021b). *Introduction to Web Accessibility.* Available at: https://webaim.org/intro/#principles.

Appendix I: Notes and additional resources for inclusive, engaging online course design

Georgetown University Center for New Designs in Learning and Scholarship
https://cndls.georgetown.edu/
https://instructionalcontinuity.georgetown.edu
https://cndls.georgetown.edu/inclusive-pedagogy/ip-toolkit/introduction/
Research, pedagogical and design center rooted in the scholarship of teaching and learning.

University of Southern California Center for Excellence in Teaching
http://cet.usc.edu/usc-excellence-in-teaching-initiative/
Center focused on evidence based learning and inclusive course design and pedagogy.

University of Michigan Center for Research on Teaching and Learning
https://crlt.umich.edu/active_learning_introduction
The center provides an overview of "active" vs "passive" learning and how to engage each in course design.

University of Delaware Center for Teaching and Assessment of Learning
https://ctal.udel.edu/
Resources from a center focused on evidence-based learning.

MIT OpenCourseware
This is a free, open source repository of undergraduate course materials and ideas available to anyone globally. There is also a podcast offering a "behind the scenes" look at some of the university's more popular courses.
https://ocw.mit.edu/index.htm

Digital Citizenship in Schools
Ribble, M., & Bailey, G. D. (2007). *Digital Citizenship in Schools.* International Society for Technology in Education. ISBN:978 -1564842329. This is a book that takes the concepts of civics, citizenship and online behavior and frames it in teaching and learning.

Resilient Pedagogy
This is an online, open source collection on resilient pedagogy framed in the context of the COVID-19 pandemic and the social justice movements that swept the globe.
https://www.usu.edu/empowerteaching/publications/books/resilientpeda gogy/

Association on Higher Education and Disability (AHEAD)
White Paper on Students with Intellectual Disabilities and Campus Disability Service explains the responsibilities of higher education institutions under the Higher Education Opportunity Act of 2008. It highlights the needs of students with intellectual disabilities.
https://www.ahead.org/professional-resources/white-papers-guiding-do cuments/intellectual-disabilities-white-paper

Flipped Classroom
"Flipped classroom" and "flipping" are common terms to indicate a move of additional course content to asynchronous time to create space in synchronous time for social learning activities. See, Talbert, R. (2017). *Flipped Learning: A Guide for Higher Education Faculty.* Stylus Publishing, LLC; Lo, C. K., Hew, K. F., & Chen, G. (2017). "Toward a set of design principles for mathematics flipped classrooms: A synthesis of research in mathematics education". *Educational Research Review,* 22, pp. 50–73.

Columbia Fair Use Checklist
This checklist helps you walk through the issues you should consider when deciding whether or not your use of a piece of content is a fair use.
https://copyright.columbia.edu/basics/fair-use/fair-use-checklist.html

Example Permission Form
This form can be a base for when you need or want to ask permission to use someone else's work.
https://docs.google.com/document/d/1L14Tq9JNM7FVWxLCN6u7GA 72YOBjEOeKwsLH1Kzzuuw/edit?usp=sharing

Resources to Learn More About Dyslexia and Dyslexia Accommodation
International Dyslexia Association
https://dyslexiaida.org/

American Dyslexia Association
https://www.american-dyslexia-association.com/

British Dyslexia Association
https://www.bdadyslexia.org.uk/

To Learn More About Neurodiversity and Neurodivergence
https://exceptionalindividuals.com/neurodiversity/

Big Tech Accessibility Websites
Google
https://support.google.com/a/answer/2821355?hl=en&ref_topic=3035040

Microsoft
https://www.microsoft.com/design/inclusive/

Apple
https://www.apple.com/accessibility/

Scholarship of Teaching and Learning Overview Article
Almeida, P. (2010) "Scholarship of teaching and learning: An overview". *The Journal of the World Universities Forum*, 3(2), pp. 143–54. doi:10.18848/1835-2030/CGP/v03i02/56669.   https://www.researchgate.net/publication/233817081_Scholarship_of_Teaching_and_Learning_An_Overview

Appendix II: Copyright checklist

ADA AMENDMENTS ACT OF 2008

PL 110-325 (S 3406)
September 25, 2008

An Act To restore the intent and protections of the Americans with Disabilities Act of 1990.
Be it enacted by the Senate and House of Representatives of the United States of America in Congress assembled,

SEC. 1. SHORT TITLE

[42 USCA § 12101 note]

This Act may be cited as the "ADA Amendments Act of 2008".

SEC. 2. FINDINGS AND PURPOSES

[42 USCA § 12101 note]

(a)   FINDINGS. – Congress finds that –

   (1)   in enacting the Americans with Disabilities Act of 1990 (ADA), Congress intended that the Act "provide a clear and comprehensive national mandate for the elimination of discrimination against individuals with disabilities" and provide broad coverage;

   (2)   in enacting the ADA, Congress recognized that physical and mental disabilities in no way diminish a person's right to fully participate in all aspects of society, but that people with physical or mental disabilities are frequently precluded from doing

so because of prejudice, antiquated attitudes, or the failure to remove societal and institutional barriers;

(3)   while Congress expected that the definition of disability under the ADA would be interpreted consistently with how courts had applied the definition of a handicapped individual under the Rehabilitation Act of 1973, that expectation has not been fulfilled;

(4)   the holdings of the Supreme Court in Sutton v. United Air Lines, Inc., 527 U.S. 471 (1999) and its companion cases have narrowed the broad scope of protection intended to be afforded by the ADA, thus eliminating protection for many individuals whom Congress intended to protect;

(5)   the holding of the Supreme Court in Toyota Motor Manufacturing, Kentucky, Inc. v. Williams, 534 U.S. 184 (2002) further narrowed the broad scope of protection intended to be afforded by the ADA;

(6)   as a result of these Supreme Court cases, lower courts have incorrectly found in individual cases that people with a range of substantially limiting impairments are not people with disabilities;

(7)   in particular, the Supreme Court, in the case of Toyota Motor Manufacturing, Kentucky, Inc. v. Williams, 534 U.S. 184 (2002), interpreted the term "substantially limits" to require a greater degree of limitation than was intended by Congress; and

(8)   Congress finds that the current Equal Employment Opportunity Commission ADA regulations defining the term "substantially limits" as "significantly restricted" are inconsistent with congressional intent, by expressing too high a standard.

(b)   PURPOSES. – The purposes of this Act are –

(1)   to carry out the ADA's objectives of providing "a clear and comprehensive national mandate for the elimination of discrimination" and "clear, strong, consistent, enforceable standards addressing discrimination" by reinstating a broad scope of protection to be available under the ADA;

(2)   to reject the requirement enunciated by the Supreme Court in Sutton v. United Air Lines, Inc., 527 U.S. 471 (1999) and its companion cases that whether an impairment substantially

limits a major life activity is to be determined with reference to the ameliorative effects of mitigating measures;

(3) to reject the Supreme Court's reasoning in Sutton v. United Air Lines, Inc., 527 U.S. 471 (1999) with regard to coverage under the third prong of the definition of disability and to reinstate the reasoning of the Supreme Court in School Board of Nassau County v. Arline, 480 U.S. 273 (1987) which set forth a broad view of the third prong of the definition of handicap under the Rehabilitation Act of 1973;

(4) to reject the standards enunciated by the Supreme Court in Toyota Motor Manufacturing, Kentucky, Inc. v. Williams, 534 U.S. 184 (2002), that the terms "substantially" and "major" in the definition of disability under the ADA "need to be interpreted strictly to create a demanding standard for qualifying as disabled," and that to be substantially limited in performing a major life activity under the ADA "an individual must have an impairment that prevents or severely restricts the individual from doing activities that are of central importance to most people's daily lives";

(5) to convey congressional intent that the standard created by the Supreme Court in the case of Toyota Motor Manufacturing, Kentucky, Inc. v. Williams, 534 U.S. 184 (2002) for "substantially limits", and applied by lower courts in numerous decisions, has created an inappropriately high level of limitation necessary to obtain coverage under the ADA, to convey that it is the intent of Congress that the primary object of attention in cases brought under the ADA should be whether entities covered under the ADA have complied with their obligations, and to convey that the question of whether an individual's impairment is a disability under the ADA should not demand extensive analysis; and

(6) to express Congress' expectation that the Equal Employment Opportunity Commission will revise that portion of its current regulations that defines the term "substantially limits" as "significantly restricted" to be consistent with this Act, including the amendments made by this Act.

SEC. 3. CODIFIED FINDINGS

Section 2(a) of the Americans with Disabilities Act of 1990 (42 U.S.C. 12101) is amended—

(1)   by amending paragraph (1) to read as follows: "(1) physical or mental disabilities in no way diminish a person's right to fully participate in all aspects of society, yet many people with physical or mental disabilities have been precluded from doing so because of discrimination; others who have a record of a disability or are regarded as having a disability also have been subjected to discrimination;"

(2)   by striking paragraph (7); and

(3)   by redesignating paragraphs (8) and (9) as paragraphs (7) and (8), respectively.

SEC. 4. DISABILITY DEFINED AND RULES OF CONSTRUCTION

(a)   DEFINITION OF DISABILITY.—Section 3 of the Americans with Disabilities Act of 1990 (42 U.S.C. 12102) is amended to read as follows:

SEC. 3. DEFINITION OF DISABILITY.
As used in this Act:
(1)   DISABILITY.—The term 'disability' means, with respect to an individual—
       (A)   a physical or mental impairment that substantially limits one or more major life activities of such individual;
       (B)   a record of such an impairment; or
       (C)   being regarded as having such an impairment (as described in paragraph (3)).
(2)   MAJOR LIFE ACTIVITIES.—
       (A)   IN GENERAL.—For purposes of paragraph (1), major life activities include, but are not limited to, caring for oneself, performing manual tasks, seeing, hearing, eating, sleeping, walking, standing, lifting, bending, speaking, breathing, learning, reading, concentrating, thinking, communicating, and working.
       (B)   MAJOR BODILY FUNCTIONS.—For purposes of paragraph (1), a major life activity also includes the operation of a major bodily function, including but not limited to, functions of the immune system, normal cell growth, digestive, bowel, bladder, neurolog-

ical, brain, respiratory, circulatory, endocrine, and reproductive functions.

(3) REGARDED AS HAVING SUCH AN IMPAIRMENT.—For purposes of paragraph (1)(C):

    (A) An individual meets the requirement of 'being regarded as having such an impairment' if the individual establishes that he or she has been subjected to an action prohibited under this Act because of an actual or perceived physical or mental impairment whether or not the impairment limits or is perceived to limit a major life activity.

    (B) Paragraph (1)(C) shall not apply to impairments that are transitory and minor. A transitory impairment is an impairment with an actual or expected duration of 6 months or less.

(4) RULES OF CONSTRUCTION REGARDING THE DEFINITION OF DISABILITY.—The definition of 'disability' in paragraph (1) shall be construed in accordance with the following:

    (A) The definition of disability in this Act shall be construed in favor of broad coverage of individuals under this Act, to the maximum extent permitted by the terms of this Act.

    (B) The term 'substantially limits' shall be interpreted consistently with the findings and purposes of the ADA Amendments Act of 2008.

    (C) An impairment that substantially limits one major life activity need not limit other major life activities in order to be considered a disability.

    (D) An impairment that is episodic or in remission is a disability if it would substantially limit a major life activity when active.

    (E)(i) The determination of whether an impairment substantially limits a major life activity shall be made without regard to the ameliorative effects of mitigating measures such as—

        (I) medication, medical supplies, equipment, or appliances, low-vision devices (which do not include ordinary eyeglasses or contact lenses), prosthetics including limbs and devices, hearing aids and cochlear implants or other implantable hearing devices, mobility devices, or oxygen therapy equipment and supplies;

        (II) use of assistive technology;

        (III) reasonable accommodations or auxiliary aids or services; or

        (IV) learned behavioral or adaptive neurological modifications.

    (ii) The ameliorative effects of the mitigating measures of ordinary eyeglasses or contact lenses shall be considered in determining whether an impairment substantially limits a major life activity.

    (iii) As used in this subparagraph—

        (I) the term 'ordinary eyeglasses or contact lenses' means lenses that are intended to fully correct visual acuity or eliminate refractive error; and

        (II) the term 'low-vision devices' means devices that magnify, enhance, or otherwise augment a visual image.

(b)   CONFORMING   AMENDMENT.—The   Americans   with Disabilities Act of 1990 (42 U.S.C. 12101 et seq.) is further amended by adding after section 3 the following:

SEC. 4. ADDITIONAL DEFINITIONS.
As used in this Act:
  (1)   AUXILIARY AIDS AND SERVICES.—The term 'auxiliary aids and services' includes—
    (A)   qualified interpreters or other effective methods of making aurally delivered materials available to individuals with hearing impairments;
    (B)   qualified readers, taped texts, or other effective methods of making visually delivered materials available to individuals with visual impairments;
    (C)   acquisition or modification of equipment or devices; and
    (D)   other similar services and actions.
  (2)   STATE.—The term 'State' means each of the several States, the District of Columbia, the Commonwealth of Puerto Rico, Guam, American Samoa, the Virgin Islands of the United States, the Trust Territory of the Pacific Islands, and the Commonwealth of the Northern Mariana Islands.

(c)   AMENDMENT TO THE TABLE OF CONTENTS.—The table of contents contained in section 1(b) of the Americans with Disabilities Act of 1990 is amended by striking the item relating to section 3 and inserting the following items:

Sec. 3. Definition of disability.
Sec. 4. Additional definitions.

SEC. 5. DISCRIMINATION ON THE BASIS OF DISABILITY.

(a)   ON THE BASIS OF DISABILITY.—Section 102 of the Americans with Disabilities Act of 1990 (42 U.S.C. 12112) is amended—

  (1)   in subsection (a), by striking "with a disability because of the disability of such individual" and inserting "on the basis of disability"; and
  (2)   in subsection (b) in the matter preceding paragraph (1), by striking "discriminate" and inserting "discriminate against a qualified individual on the basis of disability".

(b)   QUALIFICATION STANDARDS AND TESTS RELATED TO UNCORRECTED VISION.—Section 103 of the Americans with Disabilities Act of 1990 (42 U.S.C. 12113) is amended by redesignating subsections (c) and (d) as subsections (d) and (e), respectively, and inserting after subsection (b) the following new subsection:

(c)   QUALIFICATION STANDARDS AND TESTS RELATED TO UNCORRECTED VISION.— Notwithstanding section 3(4)(E)(ii), a covered entity shall not use qualification standards, employment tests, or other selection criteria based on an individual's uncorrected vision unless the standard, test, or other selection criteria, as used by the covered entity, is shown to be job-related for the position in question and consistent with business necessity.

(c)   CONFORMING AMENDMENTS.—

(1)   Section 101(8) of the Americans with Disabilities Act of 1990 (42 U.S.C. 12111(8)) is amended—

(A) in the paragraph heading, by striking "WITH A DIS-ABILITY"; and
(B) by striking "with a disability" after "individual" both places it appears.

(2)   Section 104(a) of the Americans with Disabilities Act of 1990 (42 U.S.C. 12114(a)) is amended by striking "the term 'qualified individual with a disability' shall" and inserting "a qualified individual with a disability shall".

SEC. 6. RULES OF CONSTRUCTION.

(a)   Title V of the Americans with Disabilities Act of 1990 (42 U.S.C. 12201 et seq.) is amended—

(1)   by adding at the end of section 501 the following:

(e)   BENEFITS UNDER STATE WORKER'S COMPENSATION LAWS.—Nothing in this Act alters the standards for determining eligibility for benefits under State worker's compensation laws or under State and Federal disability benefit programs.

(f) FUNDAMENTAL ALTERATION.—Nothing in this Act alters the provision of section 302(b)(2)(A)(ii), specifying that reasonable modifications in policies, practices, or procedures shall be required, unless an entity can demonstrate that making such modifications in policies, practices, or procedures, including academic requirements in postsecondary education, would fundamentally alter the nature of the goods, services, facilities, privileges, advantages, or accommodations involved.

(g) CLAIMS OF NO DISABILITY.—Nothing in this Act shall provide the basis for a claim by an individual without a disability that the individual was subject to discrimination because of the individual's lack of disability.

(h) REASONABLE ACCOMMODATIONS AND MODIFICATIONS.—A covered entity under title I, a public entity under title II, and any person who owns, leases (or leases to), or operates a place of public accommodation under title III, need not provide a reasonable accommodation or a reasonable modification to policies, practices, or procedures to an individual who meets the definition of disability in section 3(1) solely under subparagraph (C) of such section.

(2)   by redesignating section 506 through 514 as sections 507 through 515, respectively, and adding after section 505 the following:

SEC. 506. RULE OF CONSTRUCTION REGARDING REGULATORY AUTHORITY.
The authority to issue regulations granted to the Equal Employment Opportunity Commission, the Attorney General, and the Secretary of Transportation under this Act includes the authority to issue regulations implementing the definitions of disability in section 3 (including rules of construction) and the definitions in section 4, consistent with the ADA Amendments Act of 2008; and

(3)   in section 511 (as redesignated by paragraph (2)) (42 U.S.C. 12211), in subsection (c), by striking "511(b)(3)" and inserting "512(b)(3)".

(b)   The table of contents contained in section 1(b) of the Americans with Disabilities Act of 1990 is amended by redesignating the items relating to sections 506 through 514 as the items relating to sections 507 through 515, respectively, and by inserting after the item relating to section 505 the following new item:

Sec. 506. Rule of construction regarding regulatory authority.

SEC. 7. CONFORMING AMENDMENTS.

Section 7 of the Rehabilitation Act of 1973 (29 U.S.C. 705) is amended—

(1)   in paragraph (9)(B), by striking "a physical" and all that follows through "major life activities", and inserting "the meaning given it in section 3 of the Americans with Disabilities Act of 1990 (42 U.S.C. 12102)"; and

(2)   in paragraph (20)(B), by striking "any person who" and all that follows through the period at the end, and inserting "any person who has a disability as defined in section 3 of the Americans with Disabilities Act of 1990 (42 U.S.C. 12102).".

SEC. 8. EFFECTIVE DATE

[29 USCA § 705 note]

This Act and the amendments made by this Act shall become effective on January 1, 2009.

Approved September 25, 2008.

Appendix III: ADAA

FAIR USE CHECKLIST

Available at: https://copyright.columbia.edu/basics/fair-use/fair-use-checklist .html.

Introduction to the checklist

The Fair Use Checklist and variations on it have been widely used for many years to help educators, librarians, lawyers, and many other users of copyrighted works determine whether their activities are within the limits of fair use under U.S. copyright law (Section 107 of the U.S. Copyright Act). The four factors form the structure of this checklist. Congress and courts have offered some insight into the specific meaning of the factors, and those interpretations are reflected in the details of this form.

BENEFITS OF USING THE CHECKLIST

A proper use of this checklist should serve two purposes. First, it should help you to focus on factual circumstances that are important in your evaluation of fair use. The meaning and scope of fair use depends on the particular facts of a given situation, and changing one or more facts may alter the analysis. Second, the checklist can provide an important mechanism to document your decision-making process. Maintaining a record of your fair use analysis can be critical for establishing good faith; consider adding to the checklist the current date and notes about your project. Keep completed checklists on file for future reference.

THE CHECKLIST AS A ROAD MAP

As you use the checklist and apply it to your situations, you are likely to check more than one box in each column and even check boxes across columns. Some checked boxes will favor fair use and others may oppose fair use. A key issue is whether you are acting reasonably in checking any given box, with the ultimate question being whether the cumulative weight of the factors favors or turns you away from fair use. This is not an exercise in simply checking and counting boxes. Instead, you need to consider the relative persuasive strength of the circumstances and if the overall conditions lean most convincingly for or against fair use. Because you are most familiar with your project, you are probably best positioned to evaluate the facts and make the decision.

CAVEAT

This checklist is provided as a tool to assist you when undertaking a fair use analysis. The four factors listed in the Copyright Statute are only guidelines for making a determination as to whether a use is fair. Each factor should be given careful consideration in analyzing any specific use. There is no magic formula; an arithmetic approach to the application of the four factors should not be used. Depending on the specific facts of a case, it is possible that even if three of the factors would tend to favor a fair use finding, the fourth factor may be the most important one in that particular case, leading to a conclusion that the use may not be considered fair.

Bibliography

Adebonojo, L. G. (2010). "LibGuides: Customizing subject guides for individual courses". *College & Undergraduate Libraries*, 17(4), pp. 398–412. Available at: https://doi.org/10.1080/10691316.2010.525426.

Almeida, P. (2010). "Scholarship of teaching and learning: An overview". *The Journal of the World Universities Forum*, 3(2), pp. 143–54. doi:10.18848/1835-2030/CGP/v03i02/56669. https://www.researchgate.net/publication/233817081_Scholarship_of_Teaching_and_Learning_An_Overview.

Anderson, T. (2017). "How communities of inquiry drive teaching and learning in the digital age". Contact North. Available at: https://teachonline.ca/sites/default/files/pdf/e newsletters/how_communities_of_inquiry_drive_teaching_and_learning_in_the_digital.pdf.

Angelo, T. A., & Cross, K. P. (2012). *Classroom Assessment Techniques*. Jossey Bass Wiley.

Arhin, A. O., & Johnson-Mallard, V. (2003) "Encouraging alternative forms of self expression in the generation Y student: A strategy for effective learning in the classroom". *ABNF Journal*, 14(6), pp. 121+. *Gale Academic OneFile*, accessed June 28, 2021.

Awidi, I. T., & Paynter, M. (2019). "The impact of a flipped classroom approach on student learning experience". *Computers & Education*, 128, pp. 269–83, ISSN 0360-1315. Available at: https://www.sciencedirect.com/science/article/pii/S0360131518302495.

Baker, R., Dee, T. S., Evans, B., & John, J. (2018, April 27). "Race and gender biases appear in online education". *Brookings*. Retrieved September 13, 2021, from https://www.brookings.edu/blog/brown-center-chalkboard/2018/04/27/race-and-gender-biases-appear-in-online-education/.

Beatty, B. (2019). *Hybrid-Flexible Course Design: Implementing student-directed hybrid classes*. EdTech Books. Available at: https://edtechbooks.org/hyflex.

Beautiful.ai. (n.d.). *Presentation Maker: From Basic to Beautiful in Minutes with Beautiful.ai*. Available at: https://www.beautiful.ai/.

Becker, M. et al. (2014). "Cultural bases for self-evaluation: Seeing oneself positively in different cultural contexts". Personality and Social Psychology Bulletin, DOI: 10.1177/0146167214522836.

Bektashi, L. (2018). "Community of inquiry in online learning: Use of technology." In *Technology and the Curriculum: Summer 2018*. Pressbooks. Available at: https://techandcurriculum.pressbooks.com/chapter/coi-and-online-learning/.

Black, P., & Wiliam, D. (2009). "Developing the theory of formative assessment". *Education Assessment, Evaluation and Accountability*, 21(1), pp. 5–31. Available at: https://doi.org/10.1007/s11092-008-9068-5.

Blum, S. D., & Kohn, A. (2020). *Ungrading: Why Rating Students Undermines Learning (and What to do Instead)*. West Virginia University Press.

Blyth, A. (1981). "From individuality to character: The Herbartian Sociology applied to education". *British Journal of Educational Studies*, 29(1), pp. 69–79. Available at: doi:10.2307/3120425. JSTOR 3120425.

Brigham Young University. (n.d). "Using alternative assessments" (February 9, 2018). Available at: https://ctl-staging.byu.edu/using-alternative-assessments.

Buehler, E., Hurst, A., & Hofmann, M. (2014). "Coming to grips: 3D printing for accessibility", in *Proceedings of the 16th international ACM SIGACCESS conference on Computers & accessibility (ASSETS '14)*. Association for Computing Machinery, New York, NY, USA, pp. 291–2. DOI: https://doi.org/10.1145/2661334.2661345.

Center for New Designs in Learning and Scholarship. (2021). *Accessibility in Virtual Learning Environments*. Georgetown University. Available at: https://instructionalcontinuity.georgetown.edu/accessibility-2/#_ga=2.195157932.1099206096.1606092453-676118085.1597024160.

Centers for Disease Control and Prevention. (2020). *Disability Impacts All of Us*. Available at: https://www.cdc.gov/ncbddd/disabilityandhealth/infographic-disability-impacts-all.html.

Clever, K. A. (2020). "Connecting with faculty and students through course-related LibGuides". *Pennsylvania Libraries: Research & Practice*, 8(1), pp. 49–57. Available at: https://doi.org/10.5195/palrap.2020.215.

CNRS (Délégation Paris Michel-Ange). (2014, February 24). "Culture influences young people's self-esteem: Fulfillment of value priorities of other individuals important to youth". *ScienceDaily*. Retrieved September 11, 2021 from www.sciencedaily.com/releases/2014/02/140224081027.htm.

Conerton, K., & Goldenstein, C. (2017). "Making LibGuides work: Student interviews and usability tests". *Internet Reference Services Quarterly*, 22(1), pp. 43–54. Available at: https://doi.org/10.1080/10875301.2017.1290002.

CUNY. (2021). *Accessibility Toolkit for Open Educational Resources (OER): LibGuides*. Available at: https://guides.cuny.edu/accessibility/libguides.

Debelius, M., & Mooney, S. (2020). "Innovation in a time of crisis: A networked approach to faculty development". *Journal on Centers for Teaching and Learning*, 12, pp. 46–67.

Digital Fluency in the Classroom. (n.d.). *Digital Fluency in the Classroom*. Available at: https://digitalfluencyintheclassroom.weebly.com/.

"Ensuring equity in online learning – Considerations in response to COVID-19's impact on schooling". (2020, March 24). *IDRA*. Available at: https://www.idra.org/services/ensuring-equity-in-online-learning-considerations-in-response-to-covid-19s-impact-on-schooling/.

Etu, E.-E., Okechukwu, I., Monplaisir, L., & Aguwa, C. (n.d.). "Pandemic disruptions: Virtual learning the new normal for nontraditional students". *ORMS Today*. Available at: https://pubsonline.informs.org/do/10.1287/orms.2020.06.11/full/.

Fagerheim, B., Lundstrom, K., Davis, E., & Cochran, D. (2017). "Extending our reach: Automatic integration of course and subject guides". *Reference & User*

Services Quarterly, 56(3), pp. 180–88. Available at: https://doi.org/10.5860/rusq.56n3.180.

Felten, P. (2013). "Principles of good practice in SoTL". *Teaching & Learning Inquiry: The ISSOTL Journal*, 1(1), pp. 121–25. Available at: doi:10.2979/teachlearninqu.1.1.121.

Garrison, D. R., Anderson, T., & Archer, W. (2001). "Critical thinking, cognitive presence, and computer conferencing in distance education". *American Journal of Distance Education*, 15(1), pp. 7–23.

Gebauer, J. E., Sedikides, C., Wagner, J., Bleidorn, W., Rentfrow, P. J., Potter, J., & Gosling, S. D. (2015). "Cultural norm fulfillment, interpersonal belonging, or getting ahead? A large-scale cross-cultural test of three perspectives on the function of self-esteem". *Journal of Personality and Social Psychology*, 109(3), pp. 526–48. Available at: https://doi.org/10.1037/pspp0000052.supp (Supplemental).

Georgetown University Center for New Designs in Learning and Scholarship (CNDLS, 2020). Online resources: Alternative Modes of Grading: https://instructionalcontinuity.georgetown.edu/pedagogies-and-strategies/alternative-grading/#labor.

– Best Practices from Pandemic Learning: https://instructionalcontinuity.georgetown.edu/guide-for-faculty/best-practices-from-pandemic-teaching-and-learning/.

– Instructional Continuity and GU: https://instructionalcontinuity.georgetown.edu/.

– Spring Faculty Discussion Sessions on Academic Engagement: https://instructionalcontinuity.georgetown.edu/wp-content/uploads/2021/07/Report_-Spring-2021-Faculty-Discussion-Sessions-on-Academic-Engagement.pdf.

– Universal Design for Learning: https://commons.georgetown.edu/teaching/design/universal-design/.

Golia, M. (n.d.). "Course design as teaching presence in online courses" [blog]. *Rochester Institute of Technology*. Available at: https://www.rit.edu/academicaffairs/tls/course-design-teaching-presence-online-courses.

Gonzalez, A. C., & Westbrock, T. (2010). "Reaching out with LibGuides: Establishing a working set of best practices". *Journal of Library Administration*, 50, pp. 638–56. Available at: https://doi.org/10.1080/01930826.2010.488941.

Goodsett, M., Miles, M., & Nawalaniec, T. (2020). "Reimagining research guidance: Using a comprehensive literature review to establish best practices for developing LibGuides". *Evidence Based Library and Information Practice*, 15(1), pp. 218–25. Available at: https://doi.org/10.18438/eblip29679.

Granite State College. (n.d.). "Early online engagement strategies". Available at: https://faculty.granite.edu/wp-content/uploads/COVID19_TeachingStrategies/Early-Engagement-Strategies-1.pdf.

Griffin, E. (2019, June 3). "Tips for accommodating invisible disabilities in elearning". *3Play Media*. Available at: https://www.3playmedia.com/blog/tips-for-accommodating-invisible-disabilities-in-elearning/.

GW Libraries. (2020). *Creating Accessible LibGuides*. Available at: https://libguides.gwu.edu/c.php?g=1000325.

Hall, S. (1982). "The classroom climate: A chilly one for women?" Washington D.C.: Association of American Colleges.

Hanover Research (2014, August). *The Impact of Formative Assessment and Learning Intentions on Student Achievement.* Available at: https://www .hanoverresearch.com/media/The-Impact-of-Formative-Assessment-and-Learning -Intentions-on-Student-Achievement.pdf.

Hanson, M. (2021, July 10). "Online education statistics [Report]". EducationData. org. Available at: https://educationdata.org/online-education-statistics.

Hawkins, B., Morris, M., Nguyen, T., Siegel, J., & Vardell, E. (2017). "Advancing the conversation: Next steps for lesbian, gay, bisexual, trans, and queer (LGBTQ) health sciences librarianship". *Journal of the Medical Library Association*, 105. 10.5195/JMLA.2017.206. [Johns Hopkins Diversity Wheel Source Publication]. Available at: https://www.researchgate.net/figure/ Diversity-Wheel-as-used-at-Johns-Hopkins-University-12_fig1_320178286.

Hendricks, B. (2021, May 17). "What education in the digital economy looks like in America". *TheHill.* Available at: https://thehill.com/blogs/congress -blog/technology/553801-what-education-in-the-digital-economy-looks-like- in-america?rl=1.

Hopper, T. L. (2021). "Accessibility and LibGuides in academic libraries". *The Southeastern Librarian*, 68(4), pp. 12–28.

Jones-Roberts, C. A. (2018). "Increasing social presence online: Five strategies for instructors". *FDLA Journal* 3, Article 8. Available at: https://nsuworks .nova.edu/cgi/viewcontent.cgi?article=1018&context=fdla-journal.

Jukes, I. (2015). Global Digital Citizen Foundation. 21st Century Fluencies. Retrieved from: https://globaldigitalcitizen.org/21st-century -fluencies.

Le Pôle. (n.d.). *Home.* History of pedagogy. –Available at: https://lepole .education/en/pedagogical-culture/27-history-of-pedagogy.html?showall=1.

Levy, D. (2020, August 7). "The synchronous vs. asynchronous balancing act – When and how pre-work can make your live sessions stronger". Harvard Business Publishing Education: Boston, MA, USA, pp. 2–7.

Lieberman, M. (2018, May 1). "Technology can help address accessibility challenges, but many say it's an incomplete solution". *Inside Higher Ed.* Available at: https://www.insidehighered.com/digital-learning/article/2018/ 05/02/technology-can-help-address-accessibility-challenges-many-say.

Linney, S. (2020, March 30). "Why digital accessibility is essential in higher education". *QS.* Available at: https://www.qs.com/why-digital-accessibility-is -essential-in-higher-education/.

Lo, C. K., Hew, K. F., & Chen, G. (2017). "Toward a set of design principles for mathematics flipped classrooms: A synthesis of research in mathematics education". *Educational Research Review*, 22, pp. 50–73.

Lynch, M. (2020, November 18). "Why designing for accessibility in e-learning matters". *The Tech Edvocate.* Available at: https://www.thetechedvocate.org/ why-designing-for-accessibility-in-e-learning-matters/.

Matias. (2021, November 17). *NCES blog.* IES. Retrieved March 2, 2022, from https://nces.ed.gov/blogs/nces/post/research-roundup-nces-celebrates-native- american-heritage-month.

McGowan, S. (2021). "Digital learning for transfer students: From definitions to applicable possibilities", in Garder, J., Koch, A., & Rosenberg, M. (eds), *The Transfer Experience: A Handbook for Creating a More Equitable and Successful Postsecondary System*. Stylus Publishing, LLC.

Miller, J., Risser, M., & Griffiths, R. (2013). "Student choice, instructor flexibility: Moving beyond the blended instructional model". *Issues and Trends in Educational Technology*, 1(1), pp. 8–24.

Moore, M. (2021). "Asynchronous discussions for first-year writers and beyond: Thinking outside the PPR (prompt, post, reply) box". Available at: https://oen.pressbooks.pub/resilientpedagogy/chapter/thinking-outside-the-ppr-prompt-post-reply-box/.

Morgan, P. (2020, March 20). "Invisible disabilities: Break down the barriers". *Forbes*. Available at: https://www.forbes.com/sites/paulamorgan/2020/03/20/invisible-disabilities-break-down-the-barriers/?sh=58818b4afa50.

Murphy, S. A., & Black, E. L. (2013). "Embedding guides where students learn: Do design choices and librarian behavior make a difference?". *The Journal of Academic Librarianship*, 39(6), pp. 528–34. Available at: https://doi.org/10.1016/j.acalib.2013.06.007.

National Student Clearinghouse Research Center. (2021, April 29). "Covid-19: Stay informed". Available at: https://nscresearchcenter.org/stay-informed/.

Northwestern University. (n.d.). Distance Learning: School of Professional Studies: Northwestern University, "Why is web accessibility important?". *Northwestern University School of Professional Studies: School of Professional Studies*. Available at: https://sps.northwestern.edu/distance-learning/how-do-i/course-accessible/why-is-web-accessibility-important.php.

Parsi, N. (2021, June 15). "Rethinking technology accessibility in higher ed: Technology solutions that drive education". Available at: https://edtechmagazine.com/higher/article/2021/03/rethinking-technology-accessibility-higher-ed-perfcon.

Phillips, C., & Colton, J. S. (2021). "A new normal in inclusive, usable online learning experiences". Available at: https://oen.pressbooks.pub/resilientpedagogy/chapter/chapter-9-a-new-normal-in-inclusive-usable-online-learning-experiences/.

"Promoting equity in virtual education". (2021, January 6). *Georgia State News Hub*. Available at: https://news.gsu.edu/research-magazine/promoting-equity-in-virtual-learning.

Rafi, T. (2021, August 8). "Technology promotes inclusion for the world's largest minority group: People with disabilities". *LSE Business Review*. Available at: https://blogs.lse.ac.uk/businessreview/2021/08/09/technology-promotes-inclusion-for-the-worlds-largest-minority-group-people-with-disabilities/.

Ramachandran, V. (2021). "Stanford researchers identify four causes for 'zoom fatigue' and their simple fixes". *Stanford News*, February 23. Available at: https://news.stanford.edu/2021/02/23/four-causes-zoom-fatigue-solutions/.

Ribble, M., & Bailey, G. D. (2007). *Digital Citizenship in Schools*. International Society for Technology in Education.

Roberts, J., Crittenden, L., & Crittenden, J. (2011). "Students with disabilities and online learning: A cross-institutional study of perceived satisfaction with accessibility compliance and service". *Internet and Higher Education*, 14, pp. 242–50.

Rodríguez, E. P. G., Domingo, M. G., Ribera, J. P., Hill, M. A., & Jardí, L. S. (2006). "Usability for all: Towards improving the e-learning experience for visually impaired users", in Miesenberger, K., Klaus, J., Zagler, W. L., & Karshmer, A. I. (eds), *Computers Helping People with Special Needs*. ICCHP 2006. Lecture Notes in Computer Science, vol 4061. Springer, Berlin, Heidelberg. Available at: https://doi.org/10.1007/11788713_189.

Running Bear, C., Terrill, W. P., Frates, A., Peterson, P., & Ulrich, J. (2021). "Challenges for rural Native American students with disabilities during COVID-19". *Rural Special Education Quarterly*, 8756870520982294.

Ryerson University. (n.d.). *Best Practices: Alternative Assessments*. Available at: https://www.ryerson.ca/content/dam/learning-teaching/teaching-resources/assessment/alternative-assessments.pdf.

Sezgin, S. (2021, January). "Cognitive relations in online learning: Challenge of cognitive presence and participation in online discussions based on cognitive style". *Participatory Educational Research*, 8(1), pp. 344–61. Available at: http://dx.doi.org/10.17275/per.21.20.8.1.

Shulman, L. S. (1993). "Teaching as community property; putting an end to pedagogical solitude". *Change*, Nov–Dec 25(6), p6(2). Available at: http://depts.washington.edu/comgrnd/ccli/papers/shulman1993TeachingAsCommunity Property.pdf.

Smith, M., Pennault, L., Tosch, K., & Marcus, D. (2020, September 30). "Making accessibility a priority in online teaching even during a pandemic" (opinion). Available at: https://www.insidehighered.com/print/advice/2020/09/02/making-accessibility-priority-online-teaching-even-during-pandemic-opinion.

Sonsteby, A., & DeJonghe, J. (2013). "Usability testing, user-centered design, and LibGuides subject guides: A case study". *Journal of Web Librarianship*, 7(1), pp. 83–94. Available at: https://doi.org/10.1080/19322909.2013.747366.

Springshare. (2020). *LibGuides*. Available at: https://www.springshare.com/libguides/.

St. Amour, M. (2020, May 13). "Neurodivergent students face challenges in the quick switch to remote learning". Available at: https://www.insidehighered.com/news/2020/05/13/neurodivergent-students-face-challenges-quick-switch-remote-learning.

Staff, T. T., & About the Author TeachThought Staff (TeachThought is an organization dedicated to innovation in education through the growth of outstanding teachers). (2015, December 9). "8 helpful assistive technology tools for your classroom". *TeachThought*. Available at: https://www.teachthought.com/technology/8-helpful-assistive-technology-tools-for-your-classroom/.

Stavredes, T. (2011, June 30). "Effective online teaching: Foundations and strategies for student success". Retrieved March 2, 2022, from https://eric.ed.gov/?id=ED522106.

Talbert, R. (2017a). *Flipped Learning: A Guide for Higher Education Faculty*. Stylus Publishing, LLC.

Talbert, R. (2017b). "Specifications grading: We may have a winner". Available at: https://rtalbert.org/specs-grading-iteration-winner/.

Tanner, K. D. (2013). "Structure matters: Twenty-one teaching strategies to promote student engagement and cultivate classroom equity". *CBE – Life Sciences Education*, 12(3), pp. 322–31.

Taylor, R. (2021, March 9). "7 web accessibility resources every college with distance learning needs". *Rev*. Available at: https://www.rev.com/blog/7-web -accessibility-resources-every-college-with-distance-learning-needs.

Theobald, E. J., Hill, M. J., Tran, E., Agrawal, S., Arroyo, E. N., Behling, S., & Freeman, S. (2020). "Active learning narrows achievement gaps for underrepresented students in undergraduate science, technology, engineering, and math". *Proceedings of the National Academy of Sciences*, 117(12), pp. 6476–83.

Tomei, L. A. (2010). "Designing instruction for the traditional, adult, and distance learner: A new engine for technology-based teaching". *Information Science Reference*.

Toney, S., Light, J., & Urbaczewski, A. (2021). "Fighting zoom fatigue: Keeping the zoombies at bay". *Communications of the Association for Information Systems*, 48. Available at: https://doi.org/10.17705/1CAIS.04806.

UDL (n.d.). UDL On Campus: "About UDL". Retrieved September 13, 2021, from http://udloncampus.cast.org/page/udl_about.

UF Center for Instructional Technology and Training. (n.d.). *Gagne's 9 Events of Instruction*. University of Florida Information Technology. Available at: https://citt.ufl.edu/resources/the-learning-process/designing-the-learning -experience/gagnes-9-events-of-instruction/.

U.S. Copyright Office. (n.d.). "Chapter 1 – Circular 92". *U.S. copyright office*. Available at: https://www.copyright.gov/title17/92chap1.html#110?loclr= blogcop.

Ward Oda, C., Stanley, L., & Graham, G. (n.d.). "Research and relevance to the field" [Interviews]. *Capella University*. Available at: https://media.capella .edu/CourseMedia/ed5006element233861/wrapper.asp.

WCAG (2021, August 18). "Web content accessibility guidelines – What is WCAG?" *eSSENTIAL Accessibility*. Available at: https://www.essentialacc essibility.com/blog/web-content-accessibility-guidelines-wcag.

Weaver, D., & Robbie, D. (2008). "The practitioner's model: Designing a professional development program for online teaching". *International Journal on E-Learning* 7(4), pp. 759–74.

WebAIM. (2021a). *Contrast Checker*. Available at: https://webaim.org/resources/ contrastchecker/.

WebAIM. (2021b). *Introduction to Web Accessibility*. Available at: https:// webaim.org/intro/#principles.

Wiggins, G. P., & McTighe, J. (2005). *Understanding by Design*, 2nd edn. ASCD: VA, USA.

Wolf, L. E. (2006, January 25). "College students with ADHD and other hidden disabilities". *Nyas publications*. The New York Academy of Sciences. Available at: https://nyaspubs.onlinelibrary.wiley.com/doi/10.1111/j.1749 -6632.2001.tb05792.x.

Index

academic librarians 103–19
access as equity issue 58–60, 112
accessibility
    democratizing 4–5, 11–23
    disabled students 4, 6, 59–70
    library research guides 112–15
accessibility tools 6, 58–70, 98
    COVID-19 pandemic 3, 66
accountability, students' 41
ADA see Americans with Disabilities
    Act
ADAAA see Americans with
    Disabilities Act Amendment
    Act
add-ins, visual impairment 63
add-ons 12
Adebonojo, L. G. 104
ADHD (Attention Deficit
    Hyperactivity Disorder) 65–6
adult learners, diversity of 37
advanced programming guide 19–23
advanced text segmenting 108
Ally (Blackboard) 61
alt text, images 113–14
Americans with Disabilities Act
    (ADA) 58, 59, 68, 112
Americans with Disabilities Act
    Amendment Act (ADAAA)
    68, 123–31
Anderson, T. 39
animation apps 98
apps 7–8, 12, 88–102
art, teaching as 1–2
assessment charts 101
assessment design 82–3, 100
assignment-specific guides 103, 106,
    108, 117
assignments 7–8, 88–102
    designing 82–4

engagement goals 98–101
    rethinking strategies 83–4
asynchronous class time
    balancing 7, 71, 77–82
    discussion boards 67
    mobility limitations 60–61
    pacing 76–8
    synchronous time versus 76, 77
    workload management 7, 73–4
Attention Deficit Hyperactivity
    Disorder (ADHD) 65–6
attribution (BY) license option 30–31
audio, screen readers 16
audio feedback 45
auditory disabilities see hearing
    impairment
auditory learning style 62
automatic incorporation, library
    guides 116–17
Awidi, I. T. 91

backwards design 75
bandwidth 11–12
Beatty, B. 77
Becker, Maja 53
bias, harms of 44, 53–4
Black, P. 46, 107
Blackboard 61
blind students see visual impairment
breakout discussions 43
breakout rooms 74, 82, 92, 94
broadband access 3
BY (attribution) license option 30–31

Canvas 61, 73, 84–5, 117
captioning tools 63–4, 114
CC license see Creative Commons
    license
CDI (Course Design Institutes) 72–4

Center for New Designs in Learning
    and Scholarship (CNDLS)
    71–4, 76–8
chalkboard apps 94
Chief Diversity Officers 67–8
citation information 19
civics ideas 89
classroom climate 52–3
CNDLS *see* Center for New Designs
    in Learning and Scholarship
cognitive overload 95, 108, 110
cognitive presence 40, 45–9, 53, 55–6
CoI *see* Community of Inquiry
    Framework
collaborative platforms 94
collapsible sections 21–2
color blind students 113
color schemes, research guides 113
commercial use, copyrighted work 32
Community of Inquiry (CoI)
    Framework 39–40
    presence, types of 40–51
community of learners 4, 88, 90–93,
    98–9
competency-based learning 1–2
competency lists 100
conference platforms 44–5, 93, 114
content chunking 49–50
content type, bandwidth 12
copyright 4–5, 24–35
    checklist 123–31, 132–3
    programming guide 18
    territorial nature of 24
cost factors 98
course design
    inclusivity 5–6, 37–57
    LMS process 3
Course Design Institutes (CDI) 72–4
course materials, diversifying 55
course-specific research guides 103,
    106, 108
COVID-19 pandemic
    accessibility tools 3, 66
    CNDLS services 71
    student experiences 54
Creative Commons (CC) license
    29–31, 34

creative work, copyright for 27, 32
creator profile box, LibGuides 110
critical thinking 99
Crittenden, L. and J. 61
cultural identity bias 54
Curb Cut Effect 17

Davidson, Cathy 54
decorative images 16
desktop publishing programs 14–15
dictation options 67
didactical teaching approach 1
digital citizenship 88–90, 99
digital divide 3
digital fluency 88
digital learning, professional
    development 75–6
Digital Millennium Copyright Act
    (DMCA) 25–6
direct instruction 49, 50–51
directional hyperlinks 113
disabilities services 67–8
disability
    accessibility and 4, 6, 59–70, 112
    definition 126–8
    discrimination on basis of 128–9
discipline-specific research guides
    108
disclosure choices, disabled students
    61
discrimination, disability basis 128–9
discussion boards 67, 74, 94
discussion feedback 42, 49
discussion forums 42, 47
discussions, spaces for 92–3
diverse representation 37, 55–6
"Diversity Wheel" 38
DMCA (Digital Millennium
    Copyright Act) 25–6
DOCX file format 15
dyslexia 65

e-materials, research guides 116–17
embedding
    copyright 26
    library guides 105, 116–17
    multimedia 114

engagement
    components of 101
    necessity of 89
EPUB ebook format 15
equity issues 58–60, 112
evaluation frameworks 100
exclusive use license, third-party
    work 34

FaceMouse 64
facilitation of discourse 49
factual work, copyright for 32
faculty appointments, bias in 53–4
Fagerheim, B. 117
fair use
    checklist 132–3
    copyright law 31–3, 132–3
feedback
    assignments 83
    discussions 49
    video conferencing 45
Felten, Peter 2
file extensions 14
file naming 18
file uploads, plaintext vs 12
filetypes 12, 14–15
flexibility principle 59
flipped classroom model 78, 90–91,
    121
"focus order" course design 66
formative assessments 46, 51
formatting
    advanced guide 19
    filetypes 15
    preferences 17–23
"Fourth Industrial Revolution" 2
full-text online resources 108

gaming streams 93
"Gen Y" 90
"Gen Z" 90
gender bias 53–4
gifs 16
Google slide presentations 95–8
grading schemes, assignments 83–4,
    101
group work

assignment ideas 91–2, 94–5
    structuring 82
guest speakers 99

Hamilton, Paul 63
heading options, LibGuides 112–13
hearing impairment 63–5, 112, 114
Herbart, Joseph 1
hidden bias assessments 44
HTML format 18–21
hybrid learning 8, 77–8
hyflex learning 77–8
hyperlinks 113

icebreaker games 91–2
image files 16, 113–14
institutional approach, access 59
institutional support 60
instructional design/organization 48–9
intentional structuring, course time
    79–80, 82
interactive boards 94
Internet
    bandwidth needs 11–12
    copyrighted material 4
Internet access
    digital divide 3
    disabled students 4
    slide presentations 98
    third-party work 34
    universal design 60
Internet scavenger hunts 92
invisible disabilities 64–5, 68

jargon use 109
Jones-Roberts, C. A. 42–3
journal articles 99
journalism 99

Kelly, Kevin 82

labels, jargon use 109
language, research guides 109
learning disabilities 66
learning management system (LMS) 3
    accessibility options 61–3

advanced programming 19
assignment design 83
library research guides 116–17
structural design 49
universal design 60
see also Canvas
learning styles 62, 96–7
Learning Tools Interoperability (LTI)
        protocol 117
LibGuides software 105–6
    creator profile box 110
    heading options 112–13
    iFrame element 114
    LTI protocol 117
    multimedia content 109
    tab naming 108–9
library research guides 8, 103–19
    accessibility requirements
        112–15
    best practices 106–11
    content 109–11, 113–15
    layout/design 106–9, 110–111,
        112–13, 115
library resources link 31
licenses, copyrighted work 29–31, 34
linking action, library guides/LMS
        116
linking out, copyright 26
LMS *see* learning management
        system
lockdown browsers 12–13
LTI (Learning Tools Interoperability)
        protocol 117

manual incorporation, library guides
        116
market effects, third-party work 33
Maslow's hierarchy of needs 37, 39
media pieces, CC license 44
Miller, J. 77
mobile devices
    apps compatibility 95
    limitations of 3
    screens 13
mobility limitations 17, 60–61, 64–7
modular course structure 51
Modules in Canvas 84–5

MPS program-focused guide 106–7
multimedia
    accessibility requirements 114
    learning styles 96–7
    research guides 109
multiple-choice tests 13
Murphy, S. A. 106–7
music playlists 92

NC (non-commercial) license 30
ND (no derivatives) license 30
nesting 22
neurodivergent students 66
neurodiverse students 66, 67
no derivatives (ND) license 30
non-commercial (NC) license 30
non-exclusive use license, third-party
        work 34
non-linear expressions 99
non-profit/educational use,
        copyrighted work 32

office hours 93
online tools
    affordances/limitations of 75–6
    strategies for faculty 85
open Internet 34
open license, copyrighted work 29, 30
opt-in 12
opt-out 12
out-of-pocket questions 91–2

pace, managing 7, 71–87
Paynter, M. 91
PDFs, screen size requirements 13
peer review 47
permissions, third-party work 33–4
"persona spectrum" 67
photo essays 97
plagiarism avoidance 29
plaintext 12, 18
Platonic approach 1
Portable Document Format (PDFs) 13
PowerPoint 95–8
presentation-based learning 95–8
professional development 75–6

program-focused research guides
106–7
programming guide 18–19
advanced 19–23
project-based learning 94
public domain, copyright in 27–9

racial awareness 53–5
racial bias 53–4
rapid prototyping tools 64
reading assignments 99
reading disabilities 63
reflowable text 15
Rehabilitation Act 1973 131
research guides 101
see also library research guides
Respondus Lockdown Browser 13
Ribble, Mark 89
rich text format 18, 21
Roberts, J. 61
rubric sets, assignments 100

SA (sharealike) license 30
scaffolded topics 43
Scholarship of Teaching and Learning
37, 98
science, teaching as 1–2
screen readers 16, 113–14
screen time 97
screens 13–14
SCS Supply Chain Management
106–7
self-actualization 37
Sezgin, S. 45–6
sharealike (SA) license 30
Shmulsky, Solvegi 66
sight impairment *see* visual
impairment
skills development
assignments design 101
digital citizenship 89
slide presentations 95–8
social media, photo essays 97
social presence 40–46, 48, 53, 55
social presence dashboard 43
Socratic method 1

software packages, research guides
105–6, 108–10, 112–13
song playlists 92
spatial learning style 62
Springshare company 105
storyboards 97–8
student-centered approach 2, 52, 75,
93–4
subject-specific research guides 103,
105–6, 108
synchronous time
asynchronous time vs 76, 77
balancing 7, 71, 77–82
pacing 76–8
workload management 7, 73–4

tab naming, LibGuides 108–9
TASL (title, author, source, and
license) best practices 31
TEACH Act (Technology, Education
and Copyright Harmonization
Act 2002) 4–5
teacher-centered approach 1
Teaching as Commons 98
teaching pedagogies 1–2
teaching presence 40, 47–51
teaching prompts 51
technological protection measures
(TPM) 25–6
Technology, Education and Copyright
Harmonization Act 2002
(TEACH Act) 4–5
terms of service, copyright 25–6
text-focused files 14–15, 21
text segmenting principles 108
third-party works, copyright 24–35
time
balancing 51, 77–82
content chunking 50
slide presentations 97
structuring 79–80, 82
time zone management 74
TPM (technological protection
measures) 25–6
trademarks 24, 34–5
traditional teaching method 1
transcripts, video conferencing 114

transformative use, copyrighted work
    32–3
transportation barriers, disabled
    students 6
triggering events 46
typology assessments 43

UDL (Universal Course Design)
    Framework 52–3
Udoit 61–2
Universal Course Design (UDL)
    Framework 52–3
universal design 59, 60, 66
universities
    access rules/requirements 58–9
    enrollment options 2–3
user's rights, copyright 24, 31
USPTO protection, trademarks 35

verbal cues 42–3
video conferencing 44–5, 114
video creation platforms 97
videos
    accessibility requirements 114
    bandwidth requirements 11
    screen readers 16
    social presence 41–2
virtual private network (VPN) 34
visual impairment

accessibility tools 63
Curb Cut Effect 17
filetypes 15
library research guides 112, 114
screen readers 16
video conferencing 44
visual learning style 62
visual quality, presentations 96
voice amplification devices 63–4
VPN (virtual private network) 34

Web Content Accessibility Guidelines
    59
weekly schedules 80–81
weighted assessments 83
whiteboard apps 94
Wi-Fi bandwidth needs 11–12
Wiliam, D. 46
Word Talk add-in 63
workload management 7, 68, 71–87
writing assignments 99

YouTube terms of service 26

Zoom breakout rooms 74
Zoom functionality 73, 78
"Zoombies" 95

Printed and bound by CPI Group (UK) Ltd, Croydon, CR0 4YY

09/06/2025

14685772-0001